COPPERNICKEL

number 23 / fall 2016

EDITOR/MANAGING EDITOR
Wayne Miller

EDITORS: POETRY
Brian Barker
Nicky Beer

EDITOR: FICTION & NONFICTION
Joanna Luloff

EDITOR: FICTION
Teague Bohlen

SENIOR EDITORS
Steven Dawson
Meredith Herndon
Emily Jessen

ASSOCIATE EDITORS
Joseph Carrillo
Karl Chwe
Jacqueline Gallegos
Sammi Johnson
Jennifer Loyd
Lyn Poats
Kyra Scrimgeour
Carley Tacker

ASSISTANT EDITORS
Deanna Culpepper
Libby Gemperline
Asia Groves
Dani Hintz
Carolyn Jelley
Zane Johnson
Robyn Kelly
Elise Lakey
Christopher Lytikainen
Ryan Mecillas
Keira Mountain
Vin Nagle
Kristine Oakhurst
Scott Overbey

Elsa Peterson
Andrew Reister
Haley Rodriguez
Stephanie Rowden
Celeste Spink
Tristian Thanh
Grace Wagner
Benjamin Whitney

CONTRIBUTING EDITORS
Robert Archambeau
Mark Brazaitis
Geoffrey Brock
A. Papatya Bucak
Victoria Chang
Martha Collins
Robin Ekiss
Tarfia Faizullah
V. V. Ganeshananthan
Kevin Haworth
Joy Katz
David Keplinger
Jesse Lee Kercheval
Jason Koo
Thomas Legendre
Randall Mann
Adrian Matejka
Pedro Ponce
Kevin Prufer
Frederick Reiken
James Richardson
Emily Ruskovich
Eliot Khalil Wilson

ART CONSULTANTS
Maria Elena Buszek
Adam Lerner

OFFICE MANAGERS
Francine Olivas-Zarate
Tamara Romero

COPPERNICKEL

Copper Nickel is the national literary journal housed at the University of Colorado Denver. Published in March and September, it features poetry, fiction, essays, and work in translation by established and emerging writers. We welcome submissions from all writers. Submissions are assumed to be original and unpublished. For more information, please visit **copper-nickel.org**. Subscriptions are available—and at discounted rates for students—at regonline.com/coppernickelsubscriptions. *Copper Nickel* is distributed to subscribers and through Publishers Group West and Media Solutions, as well as digitally catalogued by EBSCO. We are deeply grateful for the support of the Department of English and the College of Liberal Arts & Sciences at the University of Colorado Denver.

CONTENTS

FICTION

NONFICTION

POETRY

TRANSLATION FOLIOS

On the Cover / Mario Zoots, *Unconscious Parallel*,
Re-purposed Paper Collage, 11"x14", 2014

(for more about Zoots' work, visit mariozoots.com)

Editor's Note(s):

(1) The staff of *Copper Nickel* would like to congratulate Mark Halliday, whose poem "Dr. Scheef" from issue 20 was selected by Edward Hirsch for inclusion in the 2016 *Best American Poetry* anthology; to Lisa Ko, whose story "Pat + Sam" from issue 21 was selected by Junot Díaz for the 2016 *Best American Short Stories* anthology; and to Adrian Matejka and Allison Benis White, whose respective poems "The Antique Blacks" and "from Please Bury Me in This"—both from issue 20—were chosen for inclusion in the 2016 *Pushcart Prize: Best of the Small Presses* anthology. We're thrilled for these outstanding writers and honored to have brought their work into the world.

(2) We'd be remiss if we didn't mention the Jake Adam York Prize for a first or second poetry collection, which we're inaugurating this year, and which will be accepting submissions until October 15. Our goal in establishing this award is to run an ethical, high-quality, national book prize to honor Jake's invaluable contributions to poetry, as well as to find a publishing home for one terrific poet each year.

   This year, the prize will be judged by poet Ross Gay—author of three poetry collections, including *Catalog of Unabashed Gratitude*, which in 2016 won the National Book Critics Circle Award and the Kingsley Tufts Award and was a finalist for the National Book Award.

   All screening will be conducted by poets who have published at least one book; the 15 finalist manuscripts will be sent on to Mr. Gay anonymously (i.e., without acknowledgments pages or other identifying marks). The prize-winning book will be published by Milkweed Editions under a standard royalty contract, and the winning author will receive $2,000.

   For more information, or to submit, visit: copper-nickel.org/bookprize/.

(3) Before you move forward into issue 23, about which all of us here are terrifically excited, we must acknowledge the following—

ERRATUM: In issue 22, we neglected to indicate that the Karl Krolow folio, in Stuart Friebert's translation, was published with the generous permission of Suhrkamp/ Berlin, Krolow's publisher in Germany. We are grateful.

Now, without further ado, please lean back and enjoy.

—Wayne Miller

JOHN CHÁVEZ

Abridged History of the Subject

To be born on *the eve of terror* : to speak of the *forged dream* :
to be the war machine with two names :

To exist beyond the normative boundary : to be both *self* & *Other* :
to body the clouds brightdrifting in midday :

To be recorded a footnote : to live assessed, classified, & inscribed :
to be the voiced elegy of the *troops in tatters* :

To break like day in the yucca fields : to be penned the new historical discourse :
to be the river gorge & its articulated light :

To be both text & interpreter : to be rosewater & dark blood :
to be the shadowsound of history & its volley :

To be the Yucatec coast & slave & servant : to mute the saint encased in glass :
to hear the vowel & verb & vibration of horse hoofs :

To bleed the body interred in the cold ground :
to be soiled with silence : to be time & the slippage of time :

To name & etch oneself in the earth's bruised skin :
to be heaven's edge & its ambiguity : to hear the trace & voice of God :

To exit eve's lifelust & understand the fate of the world :
to be eternity's *solemn hunger* & the stars' orphan :

C. McALLISTER WILLIAMS

A Visit to the Tragedy Factory

The purple light & the maven in the mushroom forest
gathering secret names. There is a way to speak

to memory that only the old know about, so we
gather ourselves & break into the monastery

to begin our interrogations. Not everything
has to mean everything. The prior has broken

all his teeth. The abbot has undisclosed
bruises. There is a hunger in us for bread

& destruction. There is something that is never
fully satisfied by tearing down. The light, now,

is green & gold & blinking its disapproval.
We are no longer men of the century. We

are no longer aware of our circuits
& synapses. We are the plastic

handcuffs in the pockets of children
everywhere, ratcheting tighter

& tighter. It is said, among
the wise, that each benevolent

mongrel fantasizes a mutiny.
The light blinks out & we can finally

understand what that means.

RANDALL MANN

Leo & Lance

for David Trinidad

I was seventeen
in Orlando,
heading toward

Orange Blossom Trail,
where the porn was.
Fairvilla Video,

its fried, freshened air.
I was terrified
but also thrilled,

on the edge.
Can anyone even
remember how hard-

won a little corner
of sex was then,
no internet,

no hope,
no combination?
I can't; I can.

In an
elaborate bid
to convince

myself and the clerk
I was bisexual,
I bought a bisexual

video
that I can't recall,
and a box

that made my heart stop:
Leo & Lance.
(VHS wasn't cheap:

I spent all
my allowance.)
I can measure

this adventure
in increments
of shame:

tape loop,
checkout,
the run-walk

to my red Buick
(no one could miss me),
the peel out.

And the drive home,
anticipation,
cruel cellophane . . .

Leo Ford,
born Leo John Hilgeford,
looked like California

by way of Dayton.
There was his tender
love of Divine,

that rumored three-way
on Fire Island
with Calvin Klein.

Late in his career
he raised rare birds,
volunteered

at Project Angel Food.
He was versatile:
so much to give.

And Lance,
David Alan Reis,
from Santa Barbara,

or maybe Oklahoma.
Poor orphan,
the stints

in jail,
IV drugs,
and conversion.

Leo and Lance
had the chance
to work together

twice on film—
Leo & Lance and
Blonds Do It Best—

and more than once
on the corner.
Where have all

the hustlers gone,
anyway?
They died

weeks apart,
in 1991.
Lance first,

in May,
in San Jose,
of AIDS complications.

On the death certificate,
his job is listed
as "model of clothing."

That July,
Leo on his motorcycle
was struck by a truck

on Sunset. "Chillingly,
Leo had played
a motorcycle accident

victim in *Games*,"
says IMDB,
so those who knew

his oeuvre
might have seen it coming.
After the wake at Josie's,

his ashes were scattered
by the Golden Gate Bridge.
A tree in India—

IMDB again,
as if the truth matters—
was planted in his name . . .

As I try
to get this right,
I pull up my cache

of scanned porn.
Leo & Lance:
it begins in synth,

Cali melancholy
canyon light,
and here's Leo,

shirtless,
running up a hill
in tight denim,

letterman jacket
thrown over his shoulder—
now the tinkling

piano; now's a good time
to jerk off
by the last of the snow.

God, bottle-blond Leo.
But wait, who
is that loping up the hill,

gawky, rugged, also blond,
a dumbfounded *wow*
uttered as he watches

Leo shoot? Of course:
it's Lance. Before
they formally meet,

before they go
back to the lodge
and do what they do

better than life,
they have a little snowball fight,
brief, unexpectedly sweet—

like children in the street.

Like This, Like That

ME AND JANIE AND MELISSA, we want to be other women. Not the women we are expected to be, but the ones we've seen on television and read about in novels. Women we barely remember from movies we watched as little girls. Older women. Wealthy women. Sad, married women. We are twenty-four and single and broke, but we have good imaginations.

We've been in school forever: enrolled in early pre-school, sent to after-school tutoring, fanny-patted into summer programs, waved away to college, and cheered off to graduate school by proud, tearful parents. Sure, we are smart. Smart enough to know we cannot be what our parents want us to be. So, we've made a decision. We will not be hard-working, career-focused, driven, successful. We will not even try. We will shrug off these ambitions like wet raincoats onto a floor. We will fall, together, over the edge of a cliff. Light as a feather, stiff as a board.

•

MONTHS AGO, OUR GRAD SCHOOL advisors waved us out of their offices. They had good intentions. They wished we were engineers. Now it is August and we have used their job-hunting literature for apartment decoration. Janie papier-mâchéd lists of active verbs onto a lamp shade and Melissa's pamphlets on interview techniques have been unfolded, then refolded, and origamied into swans, crabs, and Yorkshire terriers. They are thumbtacked to our ceiling with lengths of floss. They swing in tune with the oscillating fan. This is how we use our imaginations to turn one thing into another.

In July, we broke up with our boyfriends—first me, then Janie, then Melissa. They were softies, sweethearts, grad school accessories. They reminded us of our youths and we no longer wanted to seem youthful. Now we are alone, which feels right. We more accurately resemble bored housewives and lonely empty-nesters. The newly-ex-boyfriends still call—soft-spoken and full of apologies. "Are you okay?" they ask. "Is there anything I can do?" Our indifference is a fortifying tonic.

Some nights, the apartment hums with the barely audible symphony of vibrators. In separate rooms, we masturbate to clichéd fantasies of pool boys, electricians, and Fed-Ex deliverymen. They enter our rooms to find us cross-legged on beds, drowsy with ennui, crocheting tiny dog sweaters or reading *The House of Mirth*. They stride toward us, all thigh muscles and eye contact, and only unbuckle their belts once we've tossed our needles and novels to the floor.

•

WE DON'T WANT TO BE pragmatic, like our mothers. We want to be cynical and jaded. To cleanse ourselves of hopefulness and optimism. We want to be the sexy mother in *The Graduate*; the trapped wife in *Revolutionary Road*; that woman in *The Awakening* who walks stoically into the sea. In September, our newly-ex-boyfriends start boring entry-level jobs, to which we respond with subtle ridicule and disdain. They are corporate copywriters, high school drama teachers, phone-answering assistants. Unlike them, our pride will not stop us from taking our parents' money.

So, no. We are not broke. Not exactly. Checks arrive in the mail, folded up inside notes from our mothers. They write to us on free notepads from the hospitals and offices where they work. Beneath the ads for new fungal creams and fluoride gels, their neat cursive spells out advice we do not consider. *Put half of this into savings! Don't forget your iron supplements! Call me on Sunday if you feel like a chat!*

Our mothers have never been wealthy housewives. We have overworked, overextended, overweight mothers. They are on their feet all day. When they were our age, they say, women didn't have so many choices. They are tired, yet indefatigable. Our veiny-nosed, chip-toothed, baggy-eyed mothers. They live in small houses in the small towns where we were raised. They have never lived in a city and cannot comprehend the simplest aspects of our lives—the swipe of our subway cards through the metal turnstiles; the pop culture references on our comedic news shows; our trendy, uncomfortable shoes. They attended colleges, but sent us to better ones. They have framed the papers touting their associate degrees and certificates, while we have lost the diplomas from our pricy liberal arts schools, stuffed them absentmindedly into some drawer. Or maybe we never picked them up from the registrar at all.

We are so many things that they have never been. Our dogged, sensible, matter-of-fact mothers. They rarely come up in conversation. But when Sunday evening descends, we call and tell them every detail of our lives. We press hot cell phones to the sides of our faces. We ask if they are still on the line. We talk and talk and talk to them until we have nothing left to say.

•

THOUGH WE MAY NOT BE broke, and we may not even be completely single, we are twenty-four and we are really, truly, very much unemployed. We don't work; we consider it intellectually. It is an algebra problem with too many variables. Janie, who wrote a thesis on *Anna Karenina*, wants to avoid falseness and find value in a simple life. Melissa believes in patents—big pay-offs for little effort. One of these days, she says, the right idea will hit her. She hums jingles while smoking cigarettes on the windowsill—*clap on, clap off*—and stares down into the traffic below.

On our laptops at coffeehouses, we troll through disheartening wastelands of job posts full of asterisks and exclamation points. The companies hiring are too embarrassed to even list their own names; they are "busy, fast-growing organizations" and "professional environments in downtown locations." We cannot lower ourselves to these standards. We can hardly consider it.

"Make some calls," Janie's mother says. "Find the job you want. Don't wait for one to fall into your lap." But she can't understand the scale of our unimportance here, the extent to which we don't matter, the swiftness with which someone will shoo us from the premises and not return our calls.

"Come home," says Melissa's mother. "We'll find you a job here." But our lives are not fit for parental observation. We still make too many mistakes, too many bad decisions that would make them cringe or cry.

"You're so smart," my mother says, "you could do almost anything." According to our missing diplomas, this should be true, but it is not. Perhaps the system has failed us. Perhaps we have just failed.

We wish we didn't know what our mothers' lives had been like at twenty-four. It would be nice if we could not picture them thinner, longer-haired, married to our handsome fathers, pregnant, and starting jobs they would have forever. Young women who looked so much like us and had already achieved so much more.

•

IN OCTOBER WE JOIN VOLUNTEER organizations, but we never volunteer. We take up hobbies we've been meaning to adopt for years: watercolors, crosswords, harmonica playing. Some hobbies become obsessions. Melissa looks forward to hours in the day that call for meal preparation; she stands in our one-person kitchen with a knife in her hand, the stove warming her back. She's particularly drawn to the home-style production of condiments— ketchup, hot sauce, jam—foods that demand hours of attention, patience, the directions to *stir occasionally* and *let simmer*.

We see matinees mid-week with a handful of old people and high schoolers cutting class. We conceal tiny feasts in oversized purses—jars of Melissa's homemade peanut butter, plastic knives, and Buttercrisp crackers. The pockets of our pea coats bulge with the smooth, cylindrical outlines of travel-sized Merlot bottles.

In the theater, it's hard not to think of the ex-boyfriends—their fuzzy forearms and soft fingers, the sloping cliffs of their faces in profile as the screen brightens and darkens. On our first nervous movie dates, years ago, the films seemed to last forever.

Now, because things end as soon as we sit down, we splurge on double and triple features. When we finally wrest ourselves from the velvety chairs and stumble out onto the street, the sun has disappeared.

We are so unemployed, what else can we do but spend our parents' money? We make friends with the used clothing storeowners in our neighborhood—the gay men with sideburns named Bob and Gerald, the women in black stockings and vermilion lipstick. We create a new term—*hanger fingers*—to describe the speed and efficiency with which expert shoppers flip through the racks. We breeze in unwrapping the scarves from our necks, blow Gerald kisses, and disseminate, each claiming a circular rack. We put our hanger fingers to work. We flip counter-clockwise. We pull for style, shape, fabric, pattern. We know the exact dimensions of each other's bodies—Janie's long torso, Melissa's broad shoulders, my flat chest—and we pass things around. We look out for each other. The plastic hangers clack and scrape along the metal poles, the polyester shushes against cotton against silk, and we are soothed. We forget about the way our fingers shake when we try to hold them still. We keep them moving and flipping. Keep them distracted.

When we call our not-so-newly-ex-boyfriends, suddenly, we're forced to leave messages on their machines. They are seeing new girls and making less time to talk. They're too busy out on dates, eating food we would never eat, watching the type of awful movies we always refused to see. When they do answer, they mention unfamiliar names—Gretchen, Brandy, Julia. They sound so different from us, these women. Around the apartment, we laugh about their high foreheads and love handles and thin lips and long toes, about how ugly they must be. How our exes surely still imagine us while having sex. But we know what is more likely. The new girlfriends are probably mature, which we never were and are not now and possibly never will be.

•

WE WANT TO BE LIKE women who don't give a fuck; women who fuck for fun; women who, after fucking, hug their knees and stare out windows watching rain fall. But as it gets cold, we spend most of our time together, looking down onto the street. We pull chairs up to the sill, clumping like ants around crumbs. We sit for hours watching the neighborhood gentrify. At the rent-controlled end of our street, families hold stoop sales on the weekends, hocking books and records and gently worn jackets that were left in free boxes at the other end of the street. At that end, a children's clothing store is opening amidst the brownstones. The windows are strung with tiny T-shirts and onesies.

Here in the middle, our rent is high. Too high. *Astronomical*, our mothers say, and they don't even know about the hole in the ceiling. They don't know about the cockroaches. We avoid getting up at night, even to pee, so we don't see the roach-babies scuttling over our kitchen counters. We don't see them, and we pretend not to hear them, and we almost forget they are there. It is preferable to lie in the dark, curled up like infants, with our thighs clenched together. It is preferable to spray the counters down in the morning as if we're simply warding away bad spirits.

After the store's grand opening in November, the babies below our window sport sweatshirts with ironic phrases. *I knew about breast milk before it was cool.* They look nothing like the unsmiling women pushing their strollers.

We will not be mothers. Of this, we are sure.

Janie has been sure since third grade when her classmate's mother died giving birth to his baby brother. Melissa has been sure since eighth grade when she watched the Farrah-Fawcett-haired woman in *The Miracle of Life* spread her legs and birth an alien. I've been sure since ninth grade when I watched fifteen-year-old Helen Burnham's stomach swell up like a watermelon with Eddie Morrison's baby.

We've been sure since our first pregnancy scares when we lost our virginities, and all the subsequent scares after that. Since we learned to live with the constant fear of one pill taken too late, one condom applied too hastily, one man pulling out at the too-last second. We've even had pregnancy scares after dry humping, since our health teachers assured us our eggs would attract sperm like magnets. We have been sure we do not want to be mothers since our five-year high school reunions when a handful of former classmates arrived pushing their actual babies in strollers so cheap they must have been meant for baby-dolls, and Helen Burnham showed up at mine with a pre-teen.

We will not be mothers because we pity the women who want this. Women who keep lists of bridesmaids in their drawers. Women who coo at small children with hands between their knees. Women who clamor to hold babies at parties, then walk away gazing into the bundles in their arms, searching for some sort of decree. We know Gretchen and Brandy and Julia must be women like that.

"I need you to stop calling," the ex-boyfriends tell us. "I just don't have the time." Surely the new girlfriends are behind this. They must hate the messages we leave, the texts we send, our emails that still end in Xs and Os. We boost our call-frequency in retaliation. "Saw a hummingbird today and thought of you," we chime onto their voicemails.

We still get drunk and laugh about masturbation, but no longer about our Fed-Ex fantasies. We confess all of the things in the apartment that we have rubbed up against when no one was watching—the rounded edge of the stove, the slightly-less-rounded edge of the refrigerator, the couch backs and cushions and armrests. Collectively, we have humped everything in the house. Months ago, we would have found this hilarious and empowering, but now we seem desperate, possibly dangerous. When we smile, our canines catch the light and gleam like daggers. We drink the cheap wine and cast our eyes around the house suspiciously.

"Maybe this isn't working," our mothers say. "Maybe we should think about Plan B." They don't want to tell us it's about the money, but we are smart enough to know it has always been about the money.

Who have we been imitating? We don't know women like that. In our home-towns, women work as college professors, ministers, mayors, hockey coaches, wait-resses, convenience store clerks, librarians, crossing guards, dairy farmers. Even the women without jobs have jobs—they sew clothes for their children and sing the na-tional anthem at high school basketball games and measure spices at the co-op for store credit. No one seems particularly world-weary. Not enough to do *nothing* like us.

We are smart enough to know we don't really pity our mothers. We wish we *were* our mothers. Our mothers then. Those twenty-four-year-old women with good heads on their shoulders. They had a better picture of what their lives would look like, a bet-ter grasp on what the world had in store. They knew how to write checks and manage savings accounts, could bring fevers down and staunch bleeding wounds. They drove stick-shift beaters, handled raw flank steaks with bare hands, and started fires in wood stoves using newspaper and kindling and one single match. We want to be them, we just don't know how.

•

THIS TIME OF NOT KNOWING, however, is temporary. Soon I will realize this. This time of not knowing is before my mother gets sick. Before she calls to say, "I have some bad news." Before the malevolent thing in her breast is discovered. This is months before Janie and Melissa sit on my bed watching me pack to go home, watching me change. Before the hot water bottles and heating pads, the plastic pill dispensers, the vomit-stained towels rotating through the wash. Before I rise early to boil tea water, to blow on spoonfuls of oatmeal with my father, to wave his truck down the road as he heads to work. Before I get re-accustomed to driving, finally learning the importance of deliberate deceleration. I will drive so slowly with my mother next to me, that her body never moves an inch from the seat back.

This is before I will retrieve a bin from my closet, dig through the dried-up rubber cement jars and packs of batteries and the ripped blouse I've been meaning to mend, until I find the photographs. The ones from her youth. Her breasts are unassum-ing—barely detectable lumps beneath sweaters and turtlenecks. The small curves of her nipples push at the fabric of a crocheted swimsuit and a cotton T-shirt. In one photo, she smiles at the camera while holding a tiny bundle to her breast. It is me. Me and my mother and her breast, all together. Our own female family. A temporarily self-sufficient circle.

During one of her post-chemo naps, I will hold the photo between us, then take it away. Back and forth. Past mother, present mother. Like this, like that. She is an angel, a crone, a goddess, a husk. The embodiment of health and beauty and power, and a cancer patient.

•

BUT BEFORE ALL OF THAT, Janie and Melissa and I decide to try. We need money and we are smart. We attach our resumes to emails and send them out into the ether. We print copies on heavy paper and keep them in old, heart-covered folders from junior high. We remember writing our names on these folders, in bubble letters and block letters with three-dimensional shadows. We remember how we used to have different ideas about ourselves. We played MASH and imagined ourselves as grown women: an award-winning author with three kids and a silver Toyota 4Runner; an abstract painter with five kids and a red Mazda Miata; a beautiful actress with zero kids, but a dark blue limousine and a long-haired dachshund and a honeymoon in Switzerland. We married cute boys from our gym classes. The combinations changed, but there were always husbands, homes, cars, jobs. In junior high, we imagined ourselves like our mothers, just better. We thought we'd never have to try. *Just be yourselves*, they told us. *You can do almost anything.*

We wear leggings to the coffee shops and tights to the restaurants and bare legs to the bars. If there's one thing we should be able to do, it's serve drinks. "Can you work weekends?" they ask. "Early mornings? Late nights?" Yes. We can. We say this with confidence. The managers shake our hands; they will get back to us.

We call our mothers as soon as we get home. "I had an interview," we say. "They're going to call me back."

"What kind of job?" Our mothers ask about hours and wages, and sigh when we tell them. "I guess that's something. But don't sell yourself short."

When we shout, our mothers' voices get quieter. "I'm glad for you, honey," they say. "But I really can't talk now. I'll call after work."

We hang up. We hate them. We are as far from them in this moment as we will possibly ever be. "What do you want from me?!" I throw a pillow at our cheap plaster wall, and the Yorkshire terriers dance above my head. "What do you want?" My voice is not echoing, I realize—Janie and Melissa are screaming it, too. We are all in the apartment, in our separate rooms, shouting at the small boxes of wires and circuits that have been transmitting our mothers' voices into our ears. Or are those voices our own? We are a pack of wild things without their mothers—big, dumb animals incapable of survival. Our windows are painted shut and our outlets are overflowing with cords and the traffic outside is carrying people into and out of the city, but we cannot go back to them. If only we could make them proud, we think. If only we could need them less. If only we could be what they've always wanted us to be, which is only what *we* want to be: like them, like that, like something.

NICHOLAS WONG

I Imagine My Father Asking Me What Being _____ Is Like, While I Swipe My American Express to Pay for His Lungs' Virus I Don't Know How to Pronounce

It's like jammed with creases.
I can't straighten myself like Uniqlo jeans.
My head spinning like an agitator.
I guess my point being, in comparison,
you're an ironing board.
Because my _____-ness is unspoken
like my salary, we should talk
about something else, though I wish
to tell you that some nights,
in retrospect, were too limbic, yet sublime.
I think _____ thoughts, play
_____ chess, make _____ calls.
Don't expect answers straight
like your Saturday plans. Let's not talk
about convalescence, either.
"What're anagrams?" you ask.
Up bored means *be proud*, I say.
"I'm both." You're not—I'm a removed
tooth that lacks tradition. I knew
it when your pride folded, crusted
like the mouth of a needy tap,
when you first smelt my _____-ness.
Now, you load your stippled lungs
with the smell and still-bare breaths.
I imagine you asking me why I read
Sartre. Because Sartre can't reset
us, and between us, there's no thrill
but a tradition that tells me to truckle

in wretchedness, remain beside you
like a receipt, because recovery is ultimately
a swabbing of capitalism's rear end.
"You aren't like me," you say.
True: my shadow ruffles
on your burdock-reeking torso,
and my lungs aren't the ones shadowed,
computed, invoiced, item
by item, then saved and paid
for, then turned into redeemable
mileage, mane, and deer fences
that I'd pretend feel exotic
in numerous selfies to rid the thin
rind of filial debts in my skin,
though I wish I could stop wishing
someone, years later, saying *True*,
when I say what you said, so I won't be left
to feel the being and nothingness
of being _____.

CHARLIE CLARK

The raccoon in the bathroom

has been reading philosophical novels again.
It helps him pass the time before discovery.
He knows the last thing he'll be before being
cornered here and killed is a haunting made
literal. A ghost someone in a robe finds seething

on pink tile. Because there will be nothing else
to be once he becomes nothing, he thinks hard
about the yard he passed through, the hinge
on the window he flipped so he could crawl
down to eat a candle and some cold cream.

The book he's reading says the past isn't even
the past, that it wasn't even once the present.
He thinks this is gibberish because he doesn't
understand it, although it makes him very sad.
It makes him think of his mother, who was rarely

more than milk and a ghost whose back he rode.
He doesn't believe in ghosts except as something
to talk about. Her fur had nothing in common
with grass, but when the blades around the garbage
cans were gray with grease, he'd hold the earth

hard to his chest, briefly dreaming himself pink.
He'd close his eyes and see the tight white pings
of moonlight and they would make him crazy.
Had he been a mystic, he thinks, he would
have set his fine dark hands upon his eyes

and plucked them. It would have made ghosts
of everything, and so many splendors impossible.
Like the look of roses. The last book he read
was all about the rose and the way its scent
has faltered. He ate that book. It tasted more

like a rose than the rose-scented candle did.
He can't begin to imagine what the book
about the rose and the rose-scented candle
would have to discuss during their time together
inside his stomach. Though he supposes

inside him it's more hell than waiting room,
with acid for a floor and the caving red walls
of meat. When he read that line of Lowell's
I myself am hell, he thought, *well who isn't?*
The room he sits in now is like the holding

cell of a bright but unclean heaven. Heaven
makes him even sadder than philosophy does.
All the permanence, the actual endless light.
He'd spend his time there praying to have at
the marrow running through some angel's wings.

Considering its flavor, his raw claws tap the tile
like the bored short blades of a guardsman in a tower
who, seeing a hundred sudden flaming arrows arcing
over his battlement, finds their light quite beautiful,
even as the thatching of the roof above him bursts.

JENNIFER ATKINSON

White

(after Joan Mitchell)

Under the weight of wet snow
a dead branch broke and fell,

I remember, taking the hornets'
tattered gray lantern down with it.

What if I'd stood the branch
upright in a drift and set the nest

on fire, a moment's torch—orange
mark against the white white air,

a flutter of ash and unburnt shreds
of wasp paper afloat on the flames'

reprieve of lift and lilt. What if
I'd caught a torn bit? What word

might I have written there?

•

The body whirs in secret,
a mute hornet's hive:

queen, drone, sting, and a single
blister of hot red honey.

Or *is* it honey? Dare I touch
my tongue to that drop and taste?

How else to speak the hive's fevered silence—
which is to say, how to speak?

•

How to contain, to embody—or is it
to dis-embody?—the whirlwind

of unvoiced desires, powers, counter-
desires, fierce love roiling up,

rising, revving, reveling in
storm-over-the-Michigan light, flashes

nicking the polished sheen of the surface,
and still keep still at the core, wick, theoretical

axis, the scrolled calm this frenzy orbits?
The mind in the midst must stay

cool, undizzied, in order to choose
this stroke not that, while surrounded by winds

as dense as smoke and faintly
sweet in the ozone scorch.

L. S. McKEE

Cocktail

She drank it to pass a drug test:
milk stirred with a thimbleful
of bleach—at 17, the cure she'd said,
for her prowling parole officer.
Months later, during our senior trip
she would disappear from us
when we turned our backs
for a moment on a crowded strip
of Myrtle Beach and looped
the fluorescent alleys
calling her name whenever
we glimpsed bare shoulders,
spaghetti straps, a bob of blonde hair.
Our panic lulled by whiskey,
we gave up, wondering if she even knew
the name of our hotel, the Sea Gypsy,
its salmon colored cinderblocks
stacked at the far end of the strip,
where the others fell asleep
on threadbare sheets, musty bedspreads
kicked to the floor in the heat.
We were young enough to believe
things would work out.
Outside, the swimming pool
glowed aquamarine; I watched
its slow pulse of motored water
while the ocean heaved beyond,
working millennia of bones
down to glass. A place I knew
where terrible things happened;
its surface swallowing the moon.
All night, I waited for the jangled music
of a key clawing towards its lock.

All night, I waited to hear her voice
slurring through the doorway until
the sun raked through the clouds
and the phone rang and we were told
she was safe. Though robbed
and penniless. Though mournful
in the tank. And years later,
what I remember above all—how
she'd lifted that glass in the living room
of a parentless house and gulped
it down, while we watched, terrified,
enthralled, jealous of what she risked:
one step toward escape.

MARTHA SILANO

Still Life with Motorcycle Revving, Wailing Siren, American Goldfinch Trill

Still life with cell phone, sorrel, beeping alarm.

Still life with hovering flies, jet heading south toward SeaTac, 6:25.

Still life with crying toddler, catkins, arugula badly needing thinning.

With gnat swarm, half empty glass of wine, one struggling ant

floating atop. Still life that will never be a still life, will never be,

still I imagine what Dali, with his flare for the grandiose,

with his love of everything Velazquez, would make of this most vernal

of vernal equinox. If I were Dali *(jee jee jee jee jee)* the grass

would morph to a carpet of toothy smiles. As Dali, the kale sprouts

mustachioed. But no, no, too easy—Dali cannot be reduced

to floating lips, a flourish of facial adornment. Yet, if Dali got his hands

on this yard, on this psyche, he'd anoint them *Garden Caused*

by the Flight of a Gilded Flicker Around an Andalusian Dog a Second

Before the Next Siren; Past-due Blossoms with Devotion

and Longing; Poplar of the Inscrutable Conundrum; The Yellow Cedar of Ponderous Faucet. All the while the robin cheery-upping its ass off.

Dali sailing off on a landlocked paddleboard, where Dali, I'm sure, embracing

the local beach scene in a town where the green stuff's legal.

Oh, Dali.

Sometimes you disturb me. When I pilgrimaged to St. Petersburg

for a glimpse of your soupy violins, your lynched eggs, your hallucinating

toreador, *je me sentai pleine*, though a little unnerved. Always,

you were strange like Venus decked out in drawers, in pom-pom pasties,

like a white lobster replacing a telephone's receiver, initially

jarring, though really what better ear-piece to commune with the populace?

A faculty for Lorca-inspired tour de force is why I bequeath you

a yellow-rumped warbler's *chug-a-chugga-chug* of admiration.

Witnessing your waxed mustache tango, I'm a little

immortal—*un peu artistique*—like I could—when the sirens cease,

when the engines, when the cranky child melts

like a goopy blue clock, possess your fluent grace, a vibrant spurge—

alive and lime-y, drunk with persistent excess.

STEPHEN GIBSON

Improvisation on Warhol's *Campbell's Soup Cans*

In SoHo, six years after this silkscreen's creation, one year
after the summer of love in San Francisco, Gretchen W., 19,
of Greenwich, theater-major, and Tony L., 20, also theater,
were murdered in a subdivided back bedroom of a crash pad.

After the summer of love in San Francisco, Gretchen W., 19,
decided that her life should be viewed on a stage, with Tony:
that happened in a subdivided back bedroom in a crash pad,
with her body bloody and naked, and face down on a mattress.

She'd decided her life should be viewed on a stage with Tony,
but that meant nothing to whomever it was who stabbed her,
leaving her body bloody and naked, face down on a mattress,
to be photographed by a NYC police forensics photographer.

But that meant nothing to whomever it was who stabbed her.
I don't remember if they caught him; I remember the girl's age.
To be photographed by a NYC police forensics photographer
was a terrible way to leave this world. I thought so then, still do.

I don't remember if they caught him. I remember the girl's age.
I was nineteen, seeing a Navy shrink, about to be discharged.
A terrible way to leave this world—thought so then, still do—
for Gretchen W., 19 and Tony L., 20—and for so many others.

I was nineteen—being assigned a shrink guaranteed my discharge.
I'd signed up in the Navy just before I was about to be drafted.
For Gretchen W., 19 and Tony L., 20, and for so many others
their choices led them down their paths as mine led down mine.

I signed up just before being drafted, so many were drafted,
not knowing where it led, but knowing it was about choices,
choices that led down one path or another, as mine did mine,
no one knowing where it would end, hoping it'd be different.

I'd read Frost in high school: choices, not knowing where each led,
Tony L. on a floor by a window-security gate that was padlocked—
everyone having to choose wherever it led, hoping it'd be different,
like college or not, no choice alike, all of it repeated over and over.

Tony L. on the floor by a window-security gate that was padlocked
while Gretchen W. was found naked, face down on a bare mattress
in SoHo during the Vietnam war, when Warhol created a silkscreen,
soup cans like other soup cans, yet different, repeated over and over.

STEPHEN BURT

Royal Botanical

Edinburgh

From the top you can see the whole city, as if on a plate.

•

The big Chinese flora that are not quite hibiscus,
the pale striated blue of ghosts or gowns.

•

The wild gargantuan hosta
like the one that took over our garden,
big enough to hide
a kitten or a child,
way back seven years ago, back in St Paul.

•

A Japanese maple hunched over in full bloom
like an adult bending down to a small child—
no, like Snuffleupagus,
all his shade still inside him,
now visible when cameras catch him, or when the sun shines,

above the oversized, gangly, overlapping
stalks of the yellow giant iris,
whose feathery inflorations are definitely—
no, definitely not—
the hue of Big Bird.

•

The daisy, or day's-eye. The black-eyed Susan. The central egg
and whatever might hatch from the egg,
and whatever parent or teacher can tend
the egg, since hiding it is, by now, out of the question.

●

Eternal return: the scruff or fluff
across the back of the bumblebee
who picks and nudges her way across red clover,

whose wings like pedals and wheels
mean nothing is ever over.
Having been fourteen

for 25 years, I agree, and cannot tell
if it is a fact through which,
like the vascular stems, I draw strength,
or a truth from which I may never recover.

●

Plant better local flowers for the bees,
lest the rest of them get up and leave.
Dear scholars, dear
gardener: do not ask us to go back
to an order in which you no longer believe.

Cicadas

They want it to be the same thing
to be born and to turn seventeen.

See how long they waited,
how similar they are
to what they were.

Stridulation is an educational
name for their repetitive song
that does not sound, to outsiders, like music at all.

Litterbugs, shutterbugs, clicking practitioners
of non-attachment to what was their skin and their clothes—

It took such time
before they could look you in the eye,
and make an impression beyond the asynchronous
husk or mask of what they used to be.

As you sweep the rest of them off
the hood and front seat of your car, your porch, hat brim, etc.

remember why they can't help but leave
these hollow parts that were not so much *theirs*
as *them*.

We are already done. It wasn't fair.

We will bury ourselves
again, after our one
ride through your duplicitous, temperate air.

Creative Writing

The sea on its shore, for example,
                especially near high tide,
and the plain green pennants by the lifeguards'
        scantily painted wooden chairs, poles posted
in pairs, like rhymes. SWIM BETWEEN FLAGS.
                It's a safety thing
        and therefore easily disregarded,
like the fox heads, tiger swallowtail
                wings, horses's teeth, antennae and paws
in the clouds that convene or loom just below the far fence,
        the fence that keeps the dunes
from spilling and falling apart all over the gentler
                roads and beach-roses
        below the actual beach. It is as if
they had something to learn, but something that no
        human being can teach:
        about limits, about the end
of everything visible, maybe, or about
        the makeup of imaginary air.
                Meanwhile there
        are the distant preteen waders,
                the scribble and froth of shallows,
the competition or hidden cooperation
        recorded in the tracks of hungry gulls,
                where everything
        means something, but never for long
and the clouds and the absence of clouds are both
        clichés, like countable sheep
                about to be shorn,
        or only temporarily forlorn.

ANURADHA BHOWMIK

High Stakes

I PASS THE RUSTED GREEN sign for Garden State Fuel and the casino billboards for Atlantic City, New Jersey. The bridge for America's Favorite Playground raises asphalt and slices traffic in order for boats to pass underneath. Car magnets with the DO AC ad campaign cling onto bumpers as onlookers pass the barren buildings of closed casinos.

I walk down Ventnor Avenue to Mino's Bakery. For every tattoo shop, nail salon, and barber shop on each block, there's a convenience store owned by a Pakistani or Bangladeshi. They line the streets of Atlantic City, selling halal meats, imported and canned South Asian foods and dry snacks, and foil-wrapped crackers marked up with price stickers.

I lived in AC during my childhood, until I was nine. Thirteen years ago, I moved twenty minutes away to Northfield, New Jersey. We were the only South Asians living in the white suburban town at the time. In urban Atlantic City, Bangladeshis are now a prominent community. Each summer, there's a Bangladeshi Pride Festival in the Sandcastle Stadium. When the Atlantic City Surf were still a professional baseball team, fireworks would go off at the Sandcastle after they won a home game. It felt like the Fourth of July.

Many Bangladeshis living in AC are first-generation immigrants, like my family and me. They came to America to create small businesses or improve their kids' opportunities for higher education. We left Bangladesh to escape Hindu persecution.

•

MINO'S BAKERY WAS THE FIRST American pastry shop that I ever went to. I ate my first gingerbread man there when I was six. Baba took me there after I won the spelling bee. As I walk in now, the neon red lights of Mino's flicker in the window. The lights for M and I are burnt out. Perhaps that's a subliminal signal for me to say NO to the precursors of heart disease, high cholesterol, and the perpetual presence of a kangaroo pouch since 1992. At least the gingerbread man never ages.

I lean towards the shelf that's opposite to the window, stacked with saran-wrapped pastry baskets tied with curled ribbons. I veer toward the chocolate chip, blueberry, and banana nut muffins shrouded by plastic-wrapped trays of assorted black and white, powdered, and heart-shaped cookies in the neglected sugar-free section. Baba never bought sweets for himself whenever we went to Mino's. Each morning, I'd pour half a packet of Sweet and Low into his cracked cup of Tetley tea and skim milk. I'd save the other half, folded on top of the bulky pink cardboard box.

My eyes dart between the artificially healthy corner and the rows of chocolate covered pretzels dipped in M&M's and Reese's bits. As a kid, I never knew why we stopped drinking whole milk and ditched the red cap for the fat-free blue. I hardly thought about Baba's tamper-evident heart medication bottles that crowned the top of our fridge.

We didn't buy birthday cakes from Mino's. We got store brand buttercream cakes from Sam's Club with free candles. Ma and Baba used to buy me surprise birthday presents. The last one I got was an Easy Bake Oven when I was seven. I cried when a cockroach cooked itself into the ham and cheese while I prepared an after-work meal for Baba. I pulled the plug and left the bug to melt and dry into the meat.

I stare at cake slices sitting neatly on striped cupcake papers in the glass case. I tap lightly for chocolate cake and lock eyes with the mousse layered between cake sponges, with a firm layer of fudge cemented inside and iced on top.

Ma and Baba never saw snow until we came to America. During the April Fool's Day Blizzard in 1997, we drove back to our AC apartment from the Newark Asylum Office. We got approved for green cards. Baba always says I was his good luck charm: the United States issued us visas a few months after I was born in Bangladesh. In Bangla, "Anu" means bright star, and "Radha" is the Hindu goddess of love and good luck. Ma and Baba thought that a picket fence was the only protection we'd ever need. I was too young to believe.

Pale cream fills the spaces between vanilla cake layers and spreads thick across the top of the hazelnut cake. Caramel drizzles over sliced and crushed hazelnuts and almonds. Two slices of cake slip beside each other in a cardboard box, cradled on wax paper.

They remind me of the two double beds placed perpendicular to one another in our old Atlantic City apartment bedroom that the four of us shared thirteen years ago. Dada, my older brother, and I always fought over who got to sleep next to Baba each night. We never slept in the Other Bedroom that kept our clothes and Pokémon cards in drawers, with class valentines and clipped comic strips from *The Press of Atlantic City* taped to the white walls. We preferred the Bedroom with the cassette stereo that played Baba's Bangla songs and the Barbie Beyond Pink mixtape that I listened to religiously until I was eight, when second grade girls called each other out for being girly-girls if we still liked Barbies. I kept a collection of past-worn *teeps* on the wall, peeled off my forehead at bedtime. I left those constellations behind when we moved to Northfield after 9/11.

I walk down Ventnor Avenue from Mino's and turn onto Laclede Place. I stand outside the rusty metal fence of our former baby blue, vinyl-sided triplex, with the wooden staircase winding alongside the three-floor building. BHOWMIK is no longer spelled on the black mailbox in wobbly, metallic sticker letters. But the front door of our second-floor apartment looks the same, with chipped white paint falling off in splintered flakes.

I was seven when Dada and I tried to retouch the peeled-off paint. We picked up wet paintbrushes that Baba had left out in the foyer, beside a half-open can of paint. Dada's brush dripped onto my hair. We tried to trim out the white with kid scissors, but Ma saw a sliver of the moon-shaped birthmark on my forehead after my straight across bangs became slanted. Dada and I pressed our backs to the lockless Other Bedroom door while she knocked hard and spoke harder with a wooden spoon in her hand, porcelain Bengali bangles dangling on her arm. We listened to the Backstreet Boys on the Walkman until she walked away.

What strikes me as I stand outside the Laclede Place house now isn't the chipped door, the dented mailbox, or the blue house itself. It's the barren plot beside the staircase. The stakes dug into dry dirt clusters are still there, with a steel canopy net draped above them. But there are no traces of long squash stems, red leaf *data shak*, or warty-fleshed *korola* vines on the broken wooden grate. There are no black trays with cubed pods of okra and eggplant, or cherry tomatoes inside wire cone cages. There are no marigolds and mums that Dada and I had bought Ma for Mother's Day. All that's left are dead branches, cigarette buds, rusty pennies, and candy wrappers scattered on musty gray ground.

That was the only space that we could've had a garden at Laclede Place. The remaining outside area was all concrete, like it is now. When Ma wasn't home, I'd mix rain potion and pour it out the Other Bedroom window. I put Barbie bubble bath, shaving cream, and crayon shavings in a Mulan mug before I spilled it on the sidewalk. But I always wondered why the rain didn't stop after Ma came home. My child self wants to see if any rain potion is still stuck between cracks in the concrete. But from the fence, it's too far away for me to see.

•

I TURN AROUND AND SEE Richmond Avenue School directly across the street from the Laclede Place house. We moved to Northfield after third grade ended. Dada was finishing fifth grade that year, the highest grade level taught at Richmond at the time. If we'd stayed in our Laclede Place apartment, Dada would've had to take the bus to attend Chelsea Heights, a school located in a high-crime area, with a history of violence among students. None of the other middle schools in Atlantic City were any better.

After searching the real estate ads for months, Ma and Baba found an affordable house in Northfield, a safe town with a good school system. During my last year at Richmond, I heard about the September 11th attacks inside my trailer classroom with a single bathroom. The blue-eyed third grade teacher told us that the Twin Towers collapsed. Then she sprayed Bath and Body Works mist around the room. I wish she would've taught me what a dot head was. I like to take orders from an authority figure. It hurts less than hearing them from your fourth grade peers in an all-white school.

Three and a half years later, I was in eighth grade. Richmond was torn down completely, along with blocks of houses that were bought out by eminent domain to build the new K-8 school. Instead of trailers and limestone stains on a modest beige brick building, Richmond now has a three-story structure and floor length windows. Instead of the rusty fence with a walk-through hole, Richmond is bordered by thin, black gates on top of a low, yellow brick wall.

The multimillion-dollar school is built over my kindergarten classroom, with a red curtain wall separating two classes. There was one white girl in my class back then. Most of us ate on lunch tickets back then. I wasn't the only brown girl in most of my classes back then. My bobbed blonde kindergarten teacher taught me that the American pronunciation of my name was *Ana-rod-uh*. I told her my name was *O-nu-rah-dha*, or *O-nu* for short. I wrote "Anu" across the solid and dashed lines of handwriting practice paper. She wrote INC for incomplete and told me not to talk back to her. I'm 22 now, and I still haven't talked back. I'll take incompletes to satisfy the American palate.

Millions of dollars don't remember the auditorium where I won the first grade spelling bee. Nor do they remember the oily-dust gymnasium where I kicked boys who lifted up my navy blue school uniform skirt. They never caught the girl stealing my first kiss during duck-duck-goose on the woodchip jungle gym. They put a shinier playground on top of it instead.

Nine months after Ground Zero, they buried a stillborn time capsule at Richmond. I moved to Northfield a month after. The time capsule wasn't supposed to be dug up for fifty years. I can't remember what I put in it. I had always trusted that my memory would be the last one standing.

•

THE ATLANTIC CITY LIBRARY WAS once tucked in a corner outside of Richmond. I used to play Arthur games on the chunky blue-green Macintosh computer there. One day, I read about sex by accident from a dictionary page that someone left open. I can't say I was thankful for that lesson at nine years old. Especially after Ma told me that Bangali girls couldn't like boys.

I never understood why Ma prohibited me from having a crush. She tore down posters of Jesse McCartney in my sixth grade bedroom and told me he was too proud of his white skin to ever be with a Bangali girl.

Ma and Baba were the rare Hindu Bangladeshis. They held onto their homeland's conservative Islamic ideals in America. Ma had me convinced that Bangalis didn't have non-reproductive sex. I knew she was a gynecologist in Bangladesh and that there were dusty obstetrics books tucked away in the house. Ma and Baba never told Dada and me about what it was like when we first came to America. "You don't need to know," they'd say.

Ma finally told me why her career as a Bangali gynecologist came to an end, over a three-minute phone call. It was my last week of college.

I was four months old when we left Bangladesh in 1993. While growing up, Ma and Baba were called *Malauns*, a derogatory ethnic slur for Hindus. They were consistently denied admission to medical schools or turned down for jobs.

Ma was the only female practitioner at a gynecological practice that offered abortions. They advocated for women who were victims of rape and forced into sex as maidservants.

"Men came and destroyed our building. They told me they'd murder me and your Baba, and kidnap you and your Dada," she said, letting out a deep breath. "The U.S. Immigration Office still has our story."

Our asylum was officially approved on January 23, 2001. We lucked out by 8 months.

•

I WALK BACK TO VENTNOR Avenue and search for La Sorpresa's convenience store sign in curly green letters. In Spanish, *la sorpresa* means "the surprise." But in its place, I now see a sign that reads "The International Supermarket" in rainbow block letters. The whitewashed tip of the tongue.

In thirteen years, many of my favorite places in Atlantic City have closed. South End Pizza II replaced the faced-sized slices of Chelsea Pizza with rubber cheese sunken into sauce craters. Game City is a space-for-sale with the loss of the '90s GameBoy Color users. Now I'm left with Pokémon Yellow Version and dusty holographic cards that I still don't know how to sell. The Bangali-run dollar store that sold Lisa Frank is now a corner stop for gonzo porn and X-rated films.

As I walk away from the International Supermarket, I see Sharpie-drawn capital letters on yellow Specials signs taped to the glass door. La Sorpresa was here after all in disguise. I smile as I enter, hearing the manual machine crunch out receipts as the curly-haired Peruvian cashier punches in numbers with acrylic nails.

I turn to the aisle of Goya brand items. There are a variety of beans with yellow $1.99 stickers and shelves of *tembleque* coconut pudding and *flan con caramelo*. I see yellow bottles of Malta Goya that the Hispanic boys and girls in the Laclede Place neighborhood would drink. Malta Goya is a non-alcoholic, lightly carbonated malt beverage that's dark brown like a stout, and heavy with the scent and taste of molasses.

La Banderita flour tortillas are stacked on a wooden shelf, with the Mexican flag on the packaging. Tortillas de maíz blanco and corn tortillas are stacked it bulk. It reminds me of the varieties of breads stacked high on Desi grocery shelves: *parathas*, fluffy tandoori, double-layer pitas, and flour rotis in white and whole wheat. The four of us at home ate them each morning with tandoori chicken *torkaris* and mixed vegetable *neyameesh* that Ma would cook the night before.

Limón amarillo and *limón verde* are sold for a dollar a bag. In Bangla, we call limes and lemons green and yellow *lebu* too. I see the same bottles of mango nectar that Ma and Baba still buy from Bangali stores, beside dried packages of Mexican chili peppers: crisp, burgundy strips of *chile puya*, petite red bodies of *chile arbol*, black curls of *chile mulato*, and crinkled tips of green *chile pasilla*. Our Puerto Rican and Dominican neighbors at Laclede Place would bring us bags of dried chili peppers. Ma would give them fistfuls of green and yellow Bangladeshi *moris* that she grew in our garden, from seeds she brought over from there.

I walk toward the cash register and pass a stand of plantain chips, fried pork skins, and *leche* crackers beside the counter. Behind it, I see the glass deli aisle. There are signs for *pollo*, *alas* and *patas pollo*, and chicken filet.

The signs remind me of one of the weekly trips that Ma and I made to La Sorpresa, which was a three-minute walk away from Laclede Place. She had let me buy a rippled vanilla sundae cup that came with a paper-wrapped popsicle stick. An elderly East Asian woman stood behind us, trying to pay for chicken cuts. The weighed price of poultry was shown in green digits on the counter scale. Her veined fingers shook while she unraveled bills. As she handed singles one by one to the cashier, she paused for a few seconds in between each dollar to read the cashier's reaction: an open palm, for not enough. My second grade mind inferred that she didn't know English or the different denominations of U.S. currency. I watched dollars slip slowly from her trembling fingers into the cashier's hand. I worried that she didn't have enough. And that she didn't know either.

Ma tugged on my hand, as she picked up a gallon of skim milk and gave me the groceries in a plastic thank you bag. "Ma wait . . . " I whispered, as I pointed back toward the old woman. "Does she have enough money?"

"Mamoni, she's fine," she said, as she grabbed my arm and trailed me out the door. I stared back at the old woman through the glass door, her face covered by Specials signs.

"Ma, we need to help her!" I said, pulling her arm and tearing up. It still pains me to think of the old East Asian woman in La Sorpresa, to picture her walking out without having chicken to eat.

"Mamoni, I wouldn't lie to you," she said angrily. "I looked and saw that she had enough money in her hand." She let out a deep breath and held my hand tighter. "I still remember what it was like when we came to America."

Ma and Baba always made sure to grow enough *lal shak* in our garden. "Your Dada loved eating spinach," Baba once told me, teary-eyed. "Back then, it cost 99 cents a bag. It was too much for us."

•

I MAKE MY LAST TWO stops at the opposite end of Ventnor Avenue. I stare at Mrs. Clark's grey chipped brick apartment complex. It was the first building we lived in at Atlantic City. Broken Happy Meal toys and pee-filled water bottles soaked under the wooden staircase. Ma and Baba always made sure that Dada and I didn't call that apartment *our* house, since it belonged to Mrs. Clark, our landlord. She was white and overweight with wiry hair.

I used to tear off chunks of split top white bread and slip them under a crack in the metal grated window near the living room. We lived on one of the top floor apartments in the multistory building. Seagulls and pigeons would come to eat the bread ends, keeping me company while Dada went to school. He took ESL classes at Richmond, but I never had to. I think I learned English by watching Little Bear, Rupert, and the Big Comfy Couch by myself.

•

IT HURTS ME TO STARE at the Atlantic City casino skyline. I used to do it all the time, while I waited for Baba to come home from work. The McDonald's light in the distance shined all night.

I look up at the billboards: Heineken bottles big and green. Play Anytime at the Golden Nugget. Burlesque casino shows, among a crowd of scantily-clad and inebriated gambling women.

People come to AC, read the billboards, and forget them. I would read constellations in the sky and wish for more time with Baba. I left Baba sugar cookies in the kitchen so he could feel like Santa when he came home. Sometimes he brought circle pizzas wrapped in napkins from the cafeteria at work and slices of my favorite cheese with holes in it. I'd save his gas station receipts from Garden State Fuel. I'd dress my body pillow in his worn T-shirts, so it smelled like him. But I still couldn't feel his chest hairs tickling my cheek through the pillowcase.

People come to Atlantic City to play at the casinos. But I can't. I don't want to see Baba's face when I see other old Bangladeshi casino workers. I don't want to see how people treat him, or think about the drunk college kids that he sees there.

The Bangali surgeon now hands out tokens and directions. He kneels to reset machines in cheap Velcro shoes and a used work suit, doused in stale cigarette smoke after a shift at the casino.

Baba was too busy serving Atlantic City. He didn't have patients. Or strength. I don't want to see his waned white hair, crinkled lids, or the gaps and deep cracks in his healer hands.

The duct taped X's in the windows of Mrs. Clark's house tell me I won't find what I'm looking for here. I heard people forget most of their early memories eventually.

•

AFTER WORK, BABA WOULD BRING home day old sheets of *The Press of Atlantic City* while riding home on the jitney. My last memory of a jitney was a retro version from five years ago. JITNEY was written in red on top of a sea green box bus with a slanted trapezoidal face. These jitneys were a combined shape of the trucks driven by the mailman and the ice cream man, that provided transportation downtown and in-between casinos. On each side of the jitney, there was a painted orange sun outlined in white, a blue-rimmed ocean floor, a black and red lighthouse, and a sandy beach. On the back, there was a blue spare tire cover that said Atlantic City in white cursive.

On top of the jitneys, it said "Serving Atlantic City since 1915." I wonder how long Bangalis have been serving AC.

•

I SEE THE RED SLATS on the Dairy Queen rooftop on Ventnor Avenue. The bolted and chained red picnic benches are still there beside the parking lot of our old apartment complex. The glass panes still have taped, faded flyers with pictures of curlicue soft serve waffle cones, banana splits, hot fudge parfaits, Blizzards, and Brownie Earthquakes. As a child, I'd keep a snap-closure coin purse in my Barbie backpack that held my stash of tooth fairy cash. I kept half-dollars, Sacajaweas, and single bills folded inside a Scholastic book order slip. When I got to my favorite red-roofed afterschool pit stop, I'd straighten creases in a crumpled dollar bill and slip it in the slide-glass window to get a chocolate-dipped Mickey Mouse bar on a popsicle stick.

I never saw the Mickey bars after the early 2000's, but I still look for them. I hope Dairy Queen has a surprise limited time offer where they bring back the throwback Mickey Mouse bars. But as I walk to the storefront, a closed sign greets me. The tape around the edges of the flyers has browned and yellowed. I wouldn't be surprised if these are the exact same ice cream signs from thirteen years ago. The creased corners of the once-glossy photos curve down like my mouth.

•

THE NEW JITNEYS LOOK LIKE U-Haul trucks, with reflective green Ford mouths. On top of each jitney is the quote, "We keep you moving 24/7." It feels like I'm always moved, never rooted. Northfield never felt like home. Atlantic City didn't stick around either—it took parts of my home for itself. I came back to see childhood. But most of it was gone before I left.

Translation Folio

GRZEGORZ WRÓBLEWSKI

Translator's Introduction

Piotr Gwiazda

I FIRST ENCOUNTERED GRZEGORZ WRÓBLEWSKI's poetry about ten years ago in *Jacket Magazine*. Even though I was reading them in English translation (by Adam Zdrodowski), I recall being struck by how different they were from what I knew at the time about contemporary Polish poetry. Those poems appeared to have a life of their own. There was something about them that seemed at once direct and aloof, lucid and enigmatic. They were incredibly vivid, alert to the physical surfaces of the world they portrayed, yet obviously also a product of intense concentration. Even more noticeably, those poems were free of the preoccupation with historical ideas and moral questions that is the distinguishing trait of the "Polish School" of poetry associated with the great poet-witnesses of the twentieth century Czesław Miłosz or Zbigniew Herbert. This resolve on Wróblewski's part to once and for all distance himself from the high seriousness of his predecessors, and to look for models in other kinds of poetics, especially Anglo-American, struck me as refreshing and attention-worthy.

I was also intrigued by Wróblewski's unique biography. Born in 1962 in Gdańsk, he spent his childhood and early years in Warszawa, where he first began to publish his poems. Active in the underground literary, arts, and music scene, he quickly emerged as one of the most original voices of the new generation. In 1985, however, Wróblewski decided to emigrate to Denmark for reasons that will remain known only to himself but I suspect had more to do with artistic challenge than any kind of economic or political exigency. This self-exile, which continues to this day, has proved beneficial to Wróblewski, even though it came at a high personal cost. It certainly gave him the license to compare and contrast, to comment (from the position of an outsider) on the self-proclaimed "best country in the world." At the same time, it prevented his full integration into the literary culture of either Poland or Denmark. (When Wróblewski and I later got to know each other, he told me: "I'm not on a passenger boat, I'm on a raft.")

In any case, at a certain point I myself began translating Wróblewski's work, first his prose poems collected in *Kopenhaga* (Zephyr Press, 2013), then his new poems that will appear in *Zero Visibility* (Phoneme Media, 2017). The four poems featured in the current issue of *Copper Nickel* will hopefully become part of a future selection of Wróblewski's poems previously untranslated into English. Some of them are actually his earliest compositions, written in his twenties when he was still living in Warszawa. Interestingly, they are not very different from his later poems in terms of their basic feature: anthropological focus, objectivist detachment (though not without hallucinatory interference), minimalistic precision. As Wróblewski himself says, these early poems are as important to him as the ones he writes today because they deal with his common themes: radical estrangement, existential anxiety, ideological claustrophobia.

They may deal with these serious themes, but as they take on a new life in English translation I especially want to highlight their subversive humor. Without going too far into the poems themselves, let me just suggest that the minimalistic "Feel" speaks of dread that is so profound and elementary that it is almost comical; "July Air" offers a cartoon version of planetary catastrophe that nevertheless seemed like a real possibility in the final decade of the Cold War; "Hypnosis" entertainingly juxtaposes age and youth, authority and rebellion, national/religious indoctrination and sexual appetite. I don't have much to say about the droll "Our Good Old Melancholy," except that it is my favorite poem in the group. I also recommend the recent multimodal version of this poem (in Polish) Wróblewski made in collaboration with the Bosnian musician Amir Hadziahmetovic. Featuring some of his marvelous paintings, it can be seen on YouTube under the title "Melancholia."

GRZEGORZ WRÓBLEWSKI : Four Poems

Feel

I asked a certain astronomer
what makes him so afraid
(he peed on his mattress)
he replied it was a question of
distances

July Air

On the second of July, I finally crawled
outside. I spotted a big bright ball
and my neighbor's remains.
I thought you had croaked, he consoled me,
sticking a penny into his red eye.

Our Good Old Melancholy

the weather is uninspiring
sexless and very gray
the neighbors want a proof
so I show them my bleeding finger
(they recoil away from the keyhole)
meanwhile some cat
has caught an obese fly
the kind that likes shit
strangled it and let go indignantly
I don't know this cat
or who he is
also there's this constant scraping
so much scraping the whole neighborhood
vibrates
so I play with my fingernail
twist it this way and that
or press it lightly
after all it's barely pink
like a wax crayon
actually no
not like a wax crayon
more like my other fingernail
in fact I don't know anymore
I just twist it this way and that
out of pure curiosity
or press it lightly

Hypnosis

The old geezer prattled about stigmata
and his family tree (his white
horse died tragically in 1935), while we
stared at Agatha's large breasts
in the back row, a lollipop in her mouth,
under the religious paintings . . .

Translated from the Polish by Piotr Gwiazda

DAN MANCILLA

A Toast to Yanko Bimbay

September 20th 1914

ON HIS FIRST DAY IN Black Hawk, Celestino Padilla watched two men die. Although he was eleven-years-old, he wouldn't remember anything before this time. He wouldn't remember those first ten years in Argentina culminating in the deaths of his tubercular mother and sisters and their subsequent funeral processions at which he wept, not from grief but from disappointment; there were no elephants, fire breathers, or wrestling bears as Father Cantori had suggested when comparing a funeral procession to a parade, the Holy Trinity to the circus's three rings. He did not remember the momentous journey to the United States with his father Aurelio after those deaths—not the twenty-three day voyage on the steamer *Vauban* from Buenos Aires to New York, not bunking on the *Vauban's* deck and falling asleep under the Southern Cross then traversing the Equator and sleeping under Polaris, not the wonder then terror then disappointment he felt when he mistook two right whales swimming alongside the steamer for German U-Boats, not his first glimpse of the Statue of Liberty cresting above waves like an ancient colossus. There would be no memory of the train ride west across Pennsylvania mountains, Ohio forests, and Indiana corn fields nor passage through mountains of coal, forests of smokestacks, and fields of shantytowns as the train approached the great smoky city of Chicago.

He must have carried an illness with him, but he showed no symptoms while doctors and nurses prodded during his quarantine on Ellis Island. The fever and nausea did not manifest until Celestino and his father were aboard a passenger train as it chugged safely away from the prying eyes of intake officials. This was one of many miraculous twists of fate upon which Celestino Padilla would come to rely. Luck and women, rather than the cadre of saints and railway timetables venerated by his father, became Celestino's true devotion.

Though he showed no signs of illness while in quarantine, Celestino's fever raged the entire train ride west. It showed no prospects of diminishing as he fitfully slept on their duffle bags in a dark corner of Chicago's Union Depot. He slept for the better part of the night while his father worked to secure passage for the final leg of their journey. But that proved to be more difficult than Aurelio could imagine in this fabled rail hub. Black Hawk was less than a hundred miles, but it might as well have been on the other side of the continent. He knew no countrymen in this great metropolis and dared not ask a native for help; the violence and predation visited upon foreigners newly arrived in Chicago made news as far east as New York. Better, Aurelio thought, keep to themselves until they could reach Black Hawk where there were countrymen and even a newly opened consulate. But they arrived after midnight on a Sunday morning, many hours since the last of two dailies to Black Hawk had pulled out of the station. There would be no commuter passage until Monday. Celestino was deathly pale, and Aurelio could only think of that pestilence which took his wife and daughters. There were countrymen in Black Hawk. Surely there would be a doctor or an herbalist, someone who could heal or, at least, provide comfort for his only remaining child, the last of the Padilla line. Aurelio would find passage for them. He was, after all, a railroad man.

The railroad. This was what brought Aurelio and Celestino so far from home, why they were beginning a new life in this place called Black Hawk where a crazy Norte Americano industrialist had begun laying track for a great trans-hemispheric railway, its terminus to be in Buenos Aires. Word first reached the stations and depots around the capital in the forms of fliers and broadsides They appeared everywhere throughout Buenos Aries and then throughout the entire district. Each advertisement was tailored to different segments of society on La Plata.

In bourgeois areas signs appealed to those looking to elevate their station in life:

SKILLED AND EXPERIENCED MEN OF THE ARGENTINE!!!
BUILD & PROSPER!!!
in
BLACK HAWK
BLACK HAWK-BUENOS AIRES TRANS-HEMESPHERIC RAILWAY
GUARANTEED WORK!!!
GENROUS WAGES!!!
DISCOUNTED STEAMER PASSAGE!!!
IMMIGRATION SPONSORSHIP!!!

Outside tango halls and brothels the broadsides catered to more domestic needs:

FINE
WAGES AND WOMEN
AMPLE
HOUSING AND WOMEN
CLEAN
AIR AND WOMEN
&c.
IN BLACK HAWK

The advertisements in Bohemian and religious quarters spoke to poets and mystics:

WHEELOCK'S MARVEL!!!
In Black Hawk:
Good Fortune & Fate
For
Sinner & Saint

Home of Folquet the Man, Madame Lazzara, Great Fazaz &c. &c.
Healing waters!
Rejuvenating air!!
MIRACLES ABOUND!!!

Some laughed, discounted the prospect of a railway spanning two continents as pure fantasy. But this was an age of fantastic accomplishments. The northerners had married Pacific and Atlantic in Panama. Their great inventors illuminated cities, unharnessed car from horse, propelled man into the heavens. If they could move mountains and jungle to bridge oceans with a canal, if they could overcome darkness and gravity, then why couldn't they span a hemisphere by rail? And whether or not the endeavor was realistic, the promise of immigrating to los Estados Unidos was very much real as newspapers reported and—more importantly—letters back to Argentina from the first Black Hawk émigrés attested. To help create demand for the railway, Wheelock seeded Black Hawk with Argentines, encouraged settlement, subsidized their journey north, arranged to move them through customs and immigration en masse.

Aurelio removed a flyer from the breast pocket of his jacket, a piece of paper he'd folded and unfolded so many times that it took on the downy consistency of lambskin. When the boy grew despondent Aurelio would show his son this flyer as if it were some kind of promissory note for a better future, a guarantee of a better life. He'd practice his English translating the Spanish of the flyer and read it aloud to Celestino like a fairy tale. Looming above the text was the captain of industry, builder of railroads, binder of continents: Jessup Wheelock. The great man's full beard, deep brow, and jungle-thick eyebrows seemed out of proportion to his small, hard eyes. Those eyes—always watching, calculating, judging—would bear down on Celestino for years to come.

Following the appearance of flyers in Buenos Aires came Wheelock's agents enlisting services of the most skilled railroad men to settle in Black Hawk. Aurelio, a tenured road master and expert surveyor, declined initial offers from the advance men. He made a decent wage and Della, his wife who taught English and Italian in the local secondary school, was an immigrant herself having journeyed to Buenos

Aires from Genoa when she was a girl. He had no desire to uproot her yet again. But when she and their daughters, Anna and Matilda, died a tremendous sadness haunted Aurelio. Ghosts were too plentiful in his homeland. He hoped the Norte Americanos who conquered gravity and darkness had found a way to banish sorrow.

Ghost footfalls echoed through the desolate train station. Aurelio listened to them come and go while Celestino tossed and turned in an agitated slumber. Aurelio dug his watch from a vest pocket—that piece, like any true railroad man's, was his most prized possession—and set about winding it with the same care a gunslinger would clean his six shooters. They had another three hours before the only westbound train that would take them was to depart. Better to let the boy sleep while he could, even if it was a restless one.

As he did battle with the sickness wracking his body, Celestino Padilla lived through a lifetime of fever dreams. In the most vivid he was a bear cub in a den with two sister cubs. The she-cubs slept while he stood watch. When a pack of snarling and yellow-eyed wolves encircled the den he tried to stand on hind legs, tried to roar, tried to swat at the wolves, but the molasses of his dreams held him in place. The pack closed in on the cubs. Just as the wolves were to pounce a shadow fell over them. There was a furious roar, and with one powerful swat a giant bear, the cubs' mother, batted away the menace.

Celestino was still swatting at hallucinatory wolves when it was time for them to board the train bound for Black Hawk. Their passage for the final leg of the journey was aboard the aviary car of a circus train. The circus's master, Brother Underhill, charged Aurelio the equivalent of a second class ticket, a lordly sum to ride in a car teeming with a thousand monk parakeets and only a shabby palate covered in hay for the boy to rest. Before boarding, a mute clown gave Aurelio a week-old newspaper and mimed wearing it to deflect errant parakeet droppings. And as the train picked up speed Celestino woke wearing a kind of newsprint pirate hat to the cacophony of a thousand chattering birds. "All aboard." "Time for the show." "Pipe down in there!" "Greatest show on earth!" "Colossal Menagerie" "Pipe down in there!" "All Aboard" "Brother Under Hill's Bigtop." "Brother Underhill. Brother Underhill." "All aboard!" "Greatest show on earth!"

Thus began Celestino Padilla's first day of memory.

Through cracks in the boxcar's slat walls, Celestino watched the landscape change from crowded city, to shantytown, to marshland, to farm, to meadow, to forest. "When will we be there?" he asked his father.

Aurelio checked his watch, timed the passing of a mile marker to calculate their speed, and gave the age-old answer parents give to such questions: "Soon." He unclasped his watch from its chain and handed it to his son. "Try to keep time as I showed you, Tino. Mark at the next milepost."

It was difficult for Celestino to concentrate on the movement of the watch and passing signposts without feeling the bile in his stomach churn, but eventually the passing tableau—maple and elm arboring the track to form a viridescent tunnel, rippled sunlight glinting off the Fox River, a lonesome cabin on the river's far bank, an abandoned hobo jungle on the near, a spooked deer, a trout-diving eagle—transfixed and soothed him. In short time the farms and the shanty towns began to re-appear. The train diverged from the river and crested a ridge. Spires and smokestacks, row houses and warehouses, parks and gardens, ramshackle hovels and stately Victorians fanned out from the river in every direction.

When the train finally descended into the city Celestino saw hundreds of people lining the roadbed. They waved as the train steamed into St. Rita's Station, cheered as if it transported a victorious army returned from battle. Celestino would always think back to their arrival in Black Hawk aboard Brother Underhill's circus train and remember how he just knew that the cheers were for him and his father. Rather than simply arriving at the terminus of a 6,000 mile migration, the ovation gave him the feeling of homecoming. And he could not know it, for he had no memory left, but the arrival aboard the circus train was every bit the spectacle he'd been promised when Father Cantori prepared him for his mother and sisters' funeral processions.

Crowds take on a singular face, be it joyful or fearful, grief-stricken or enraptured, and it becomes impossible to distinguish individuals. But on this day, when all of Black Hawk turned out to welcome Celestino, cheering wildly, tossing bouquets and streamers at the train, one face stood out to the boy. He had no words for what he saw or felt; he had yet to acquire the aesthetic vocabulary or libidinal vitality necessary to describe a woman of her stature. Pretty or beautiful would not suffice, nor exciting, powerful, magnificent, awe-inspiring. Perhaps he would have chosen shimmering and smoldering had he the words. Even if she weren't wearing a form-fitting corset-less gown, even if that gown weren't purple inlayed with gold lamé while everyone else around her seemed to be draped in hues of gray, even if her brown-black hair and dark eyes hadn't so contrasted her ivory skin, even if she wasn't standing on a dais next fellow Third Ward dignitaries she would have commanded his attention.

Because Celestino Padilla was pulled into her orbit so immediately and completely he didn't notice the six monk parakeets that escaped the aviary car when the mute clown-turned-porter failed to latch the door after the Padillas disembarked. And when Celestino finally did notice the birds, they were no longer birds but a green-feathered halo circling the extra-ordinary woman for whom he had no vocabulary to describe. This, on a day of novelty, was Celestino's first impression of Olivia Ottoni.

She was less a muse than she was a force of nature. The great tango dancer arrived in Black Hawk a year before at the age of sixteen in a private Pullman car courtesy of Wheelock Enterprises. In her possession were 131 steamer trunks, 100 of which were rumored to be filled with dancing shoes, for Olivia Ottoni danced with such power and lust that she wore out shoes faster than Black Hawk butchers wore down cleaver blades. By that time she'd already declined offers of marriage from European princes, South American generals, and a hundred other men—great and small—who all fell under her enchantment as she danced tangos and flamencos at the fabled Club Labrador in Buenos Aires. And when, finally, one of those men managed to touch her, it was not with charm or wit or pocketbook, but with a grand gesture.

Jessup Wheelock, more than twice her age, was not the handsomest, richest, kindest, or smartest of her suitors. He was not even single. The man was married with twin sons scarcely younger than her. It was for the railway he promised in a haze of love that Olivia Ottoni gave up fame in her homeland and journeyed north. She insisted on travelling overland because Olivia Ottoni feared and despised the sea. She spent her first ten years in a Patagonian fishing village at the end of the world where the sea claimed the lives of her father and uncle and brothers, of every man she loved. But her desire to see the north rivaled her contempt for the sea. And so before a golden spike would ever be set, before a scant 100 miles of track were laid in either direction, she made Wheelock promise to build a station, a grand terminal for the railway in Buenos Aires. And only when she saw that construction on the station had begun did Olivia Ottoni embark on the perilous 6,000 mile journey, encountering revolutions, surviving earthquakes, and weathering python blights along the way.

Word spread quickly of her arrival, for how could such a woman go unnoticed? Patrons travelled from Chicago and Milwaukee and well beyond to catch one of her performances at Club Beiderbecke. Townsfolk gave her special favor, and in the Third Ward regarded her with as much, if not more, respect than Alderman Boss Figgis, ironworkers union president Aldo Kushner, or Monsignor Fermoy.

Like its counterpart in Buenos Aires, the magnificent Black Hawk station being erected in Olivia Ottoni's honor was far from complete, but day by day it rose. From St. Rita's station Aurelio could make out scaffolding and cranes in the distance. He opened his flyer, studied the artist's rendering of Wheelock's station and the city's geography, pointed north to the construction. "There, Tino. Do you see? That's the railway. That's our purpose." Aurelio was so transfixed on the grand station taking shape in the distance that he didn't see the boy collapse.

Of course not a soul in the crowd at St. Rita's Station noticed Celestino's collapse either. Mother Bontemps, the lion tamer, had unloaded her grandest cats, Charlemagne and Leona, and made them roar at the whip of a switch to put a fright into the spectators. The only one to see him collapse was Olivia Ottoni.

She sprang from the dais and glided through the crowd, slicing between them more deftly than she would cut a path on the dance floor. Monk parakeets haloed her the entire way. Aurelio cradled Celestino, and when she reached them Olivia palmed the boy's forehead. Her hand was cool compared to his fever-skin. It was a particular chill which would have been noticeable on the skin of a healthy person in winter. It came from growing up at the end of the earth, a chill she channeled from her men who met frigid deaths in watery graves. It was an iciness that complemented the fiery tangos and flamencos she danced, those exhibitions of artistry and passion which consumed her, which burned her to the ground each night.

She smiled at Celestino, not the smile of a nursemaid or mother, but that of a dancer finding her rhythm. "Madame Lazzara will know what to do," she told Aurelio in the Italianate Spanish of their homeland and led them through the crowd. They turned from St. Rita's station onto Sulaco Avenue and hurried past the Salzach Tavern and Moser's Jeweler toward the Fox River then down a rickety staircase to an abandoned avenue which ran under timber pilings supporting a boardwalk. This darkened alley known to Black Hawkers as Turk Street wound a length of the riverfront from Sulaco Avenue six blocks north to the LaSalle Ironworks.

They passed fishmongers hawking catches from the river, a bazaar selling everything from dry goods and oils to flamenco guitars and Gypsy lutes, vendors of smoked meats and vendors of candied apples, ice merchants, bate shops. As they ventured along Turk Street deeper into the shadows, they passed closet-sized shacks housing entire families—five and six souls under one roof, money lenders, dentists, opium and gambling dens, taverns with names like *River Rat* and *Sawknuckle.*

Olivia Ottoni led them to *Hermanas de la Plata,* one of several Turk Street brothels. Aurelio paused before they set foot on the front porch. What kind of corruption awaited his son? "We're not here for amusements," Olivia Ottoni reassured the father. "The Madame Lazzara resides here." She rattled a series of knocks on the door. Paused. Repeated the pattern.

The door opened to a soft pink light and the scent of licorice and juniper, a stark contrast to the sawdust and vomit odor emanating from the taverns they'd passed. The pleasing aroma and warm light roused Celestino enough to take note of his surroundings. He had no concept of a house of prostitution, so he didn't see the women for their occupation. He saw beautiful, bored-looking women, women who looked familiar to him, who shared his mother's and sisters' aquiline noses and high cheeks. These women were of no relation, but this was a Porteño house and there was a regional familiarity. In the back of the house, where a kitchen would have been, a purple tent had been set up. The black chimney of a stove pipe poked out its top and ran through a wall. Olivia Ottoni told the father and son to wait and disappeared into the tent. After what felt like hours to Celestino, but no more than a minute according to his father's timepiece which the boy still held tight, Olivia parted the flaps and beckoned them in.

Madame Lazzara was not a Gypsy. Nor was she an Argentine. She considered herself native. This she would loudly declare in broken English when discussing the newest wave of immigrants to the city. "I been in Black Hawk many years past this. I'm the real." In fact, no one knew from which corner of the globe the Madame hailed or where she acquired her healing powers. All that was certain was that the Madame's skill in the healing arts was unrivaled. The typhoid fever which plagued the city the previous year claimed none of those under her care. It was well known that the pitchers of the Black Hawk Tomahawks pooled a year's salary to acquire a balm which, when rubbed into their arms, made curveballs dance like charmed cobras; that summer the Tomahawks lost a scant four games on their way to the Iron League's championship. And the prostitutes at *Hermanas de la Plata*, all under the Madame's care, were the epitome of health, a miracle for any residents of Turk Street, let alone for public women.

When they entered the den Madame Lazzara nodded to Olivia and motioned Aurelio to place Celestino on the cot by her side. She lit a cigarette off the stove then inserted the butt end into Celestino's ear. She gently blew until it glowed orange and a clove smoke, that flavor of tobacco favored by residents of Black Hawk's Third Ward—gadjo and Gypsy alike—overtook the den. She boiled a poultice of garlic and chili pepper and a secret ingredient poured from a blue jar then wrapped linen soaked in the mixture around the boy. When Celestino's cheeks reddened and his eyes opened wide Aurelio prayed benediction.

"Bank prayers for your desperations," warned Madame Lazzara. "My work is proven. The boy will sleep and sweat the sickness away."

Olivia Ottoni bent down and kissed Celestino on the forehead. Her lips were as cool as her palm, a luxurious sensation that Celestino would never forget. "Live long enough to break many hearts," she whispered to him. She thanked the Madame and slipped folding money into her pocket.

Because he was Argentine, she correctly assumed Aurelio was in Black Hawk to work the railroad. Olivia Ottoni gave Aurelio a card advertising Club Beiderbecke's burlesque and tango shows. "If you can't find your contact near the station, look for him at my club. When Wheelock's men hold two dollars in the pocket, they'll find a way to spend three." And then Olivia Ottoni glided out the tent.

If not the Madame's remedy or Olivia's kiss, it could have been the shock of what occurred next that fully revived Celestino.

Many hours after Olivia Ottoni departed and well after the last of the Madame's clove cigarettes burned out, there was a commotion in the front of the house. A thunderous rapping on the door preceded a chorus of angry men who shouted curses in various languages and kicked open bedroom doors. Women screamed and johns scampered. Furniture toppled. Glass shattered.

When Celestino woke to this uproar Madame Lazzara was nowhere to be found. Aurelio led his revived son by the hand down a hallway. Just as they reached the kicked in front door the mob which ransacked the house emerged from one of the bedrooms with a battered, one-handed man in their clutches. Celestino and Aurelio were swept up in the tide of the mob as it paraded the man out of the brothel, down Turk Street and across Sulaco Avenue onto Pere Marquette Boulevard, streets Celestino Padilla would come to know like the fortune lines on his palm.

The one-handed man's name was Yanko Bimbay and his would be the first death Celestino Padilla witnessed that day. Yanko Bimbay, habitual pickpocket, was no stranger to Third Ward justice as evidenced by his missing right hand which had been loped off in one swift hack of a meat cutter's cleaver. But this time it was not as much what he robbed, but how the thief celebrated his heists which proved to be the greater offense. Yanko, a Bimbay Gypsy of fair complexion, was known to pass as white and frequent gadjo brothels like *Hermanas*. This defiling of white women, even though they were of a public variety, was more unforgivable to the mob than the thieving.

And so the mob paraded the one-handed Gypsy to a makeshift gallows in the shadows of the New Era stock yard where a hangman's noose dangled off the arm of a street lamp. A barrel stood beneath the noose. A meat cutter-turned-hangman by the name of Slavoj Duda offered his bottle of rum to the crowd. "A toast to Yanko Bimbay, who defeated us for the last time!"

"To Yanko Bimbay!" shouted the mob in reply then broke into a round of cheers. Celestino, marveling at the spectacle but not knowing what they were cheering for, clapped along with the vengeful crowd until his father clasped both the boy's hands in one of his enormous ones and covered his eyes with the other. But Celestino could see through his father's fingers just as he'd been able to look upon the world through the slat walls of the train car. He watched the mob stand the beaten man on the barrel beneath the rope. Then Duda climbed a ladder and cinched the noose around the Gypsy's neck. When Duda climbed down a hush came over the mob and Yanko Bimbay spoke. The words were unfamiliar to Celestino. Not the Spanish he grew up speaking, not the angular English or the florid Italian his mother taught him. The Gypsy spoke in the Kalderash dialect of Romani used by the Bimbay clan. And after spitting words in his native tongue Yanko translated for the gadjos. "A curse upon this crowd of vulgars for three generations. May you live to see your grandchildren perish. May your Godforsaken city burn. *Phabárdyol!*" And just as the Gypsy's word for burn escaped his lips, Slavoj Duda kicked the barrel out from Yanko Bimbay's feet. There was a snap—the rope or the man's neck—and the hanged man swung. Feet twitched. A shoe kicked off. One last bit of life trashed from the core of his being, then an evacuation, then nothing. And the mob cheered once more.

Gypsies from Yanko's kumpania dared to gather near the crowd of gadjos celebrating the lynching. Though they had come to accept the abuse as a matter of dealing with these people, they could not abide this, the lynching of their brother. Yanko, by no means an innocent man, still deserved better, deserved a natural death or, at least, one met out by his own people. The reveling mob paid the Bimbays on their fringe no mind as they passed bottles, sang songs, and lit firecrackers.

And just as the last of Yanko's essence dripped down his legs, pooling around the shoe which had slipped off, one Gypsy—a boy, Celestino noted, not much older than he—lit a rag stemming from a bottle filled with amber liquid and tossed it over the crowd. The bottle tumbled end over end in a high arc dripping a comet tail of glowing ash. The bottle smashed against the lamppost from which Yanko Bimbay swung and flame ran down the post to engulf the rope and then the dead man. The crowd—spectators, vigilantes, and Gypsies alike—broke and ran for their lives when two then three then four more bottles smashed against a La Mancha beer advertisement towering over the street and sent the billboard up in flames.

There was a terrible groan as the timber of the billboard gave way and collapsed into the frenzied crowd. Shouts and screams. Police whistles. Bell-clanging fire engines. Aurelio hefted Celestino over his shoulder and barreled through the crowds while managing to dodge flying rocks and club-swinging constables. When there was enough room, Aurelio put his son down and led him by the hand down the smoky streets. The rapid clanging of another bell sounded in the distance then grew closer and closer until almost immediately it was upon them. Light broke through the smoke. Iron ground against iron. Aurelio knew that terrible sound all too well as the wheel break of a car on rail. And then a thud and Celestino no longer felt his father's grip, and another thud. And when the smoke cleared and the street car passed Aurelio Padilla lay mangled and lifeless on the tracks.

Whatever grace spared young Celestino the memory of the grief he knew when his mother and sisters perished, whatever bargain the fates made with him to deaden that heartbreak, a terrible, unremitting presence now bore upon him a hundredfold. For the rest of his days he would know this moment, see it in dreams and in waking life. Visions always bubbling to the surface. Visions he would attempt to chase away with women and liquor, with tests of combat and games of chance. Visions which he would allow to wash over him in the darkest of times, to embrace, to challenge, to probe as if he were dragging his tongue over a decayed tooth, mining for a nerve, searching for that exquisite, electric shock at the moment of discovery: the river of blood snaking and oxbowing away from his father in a perfect crimson model of the river they followed into town that morning. The final sputter of breath from his father's mouth, not a protest or sigh of relief, nothing more or less than a release. The two day's stubble on his face. The chipped front tooth. The scar on his left cheek, the one Celestino never bothered to learn the story behind. The eyes, blue-gray, frozen in a final lament, looking beyond Celestino, looking to the future, looking to the scaffold and cranes erecting Jessup Wheelock's magnificent, foolhardy railway.

HANNAH CRAIG

You Know I'm Right to Do So

This week I realized that I'd forgotten the names of everyone
I ever knew who made meth. *Cooked* it, like it was a curry.

Like it was broth or marrow. I forgot their names and what
I was doing with them, those chemists in plaid shirts and jeans.

I forgot their names and their quiet dissipation, how they went
from names into shadows and from there, into chairs

in the cooling November courtyard at the university.
Which is where I had gone to live. Which was already between us

and changing everything. I forget that saying goodbye seemed
for sure like the last time and was.

O I was vicious with all that indifference and felt it.
And now I forget.

How it feels to turn out of the Enchanted Hills trailer park
onto the county road. The negative space of a trillion uncounted

organisms, riding the rods of heat and light, spitting out electrons
with amazing fury. And the pickling smell on that plaid shirt, the odor

of adhesion and dilution. The hairline fracture between
car window and nightlight into which my breath

would go, carrying out all its dire smoke. And now,
to use them, the makers of meth, the Indiana boys,

the kings of hard-science that I could not fathom. To use them
after having bested them. And still, somehow, to lose them.

JEFF HARDIN

This Thing That Has Happened

The writers
            are placing children into texts,
dropping them from great heights,
washing them up on shores
                              where adults walk,
finding them in remote places where killers
thought no one, for generations, if ever,
                                          would look.

                        •

One fell off a boat, another wandered into traffic,
another
            wondered what would happen if . . .

                        •

The dog leapt at the one girl's throat
before the neighbors,
                        who are understandably distraught,
could pull the insane thing off.

                        •

Lying there,
            the girl appeared to be saying something,
mouthing her own blood, gasping,
but no one present could make the words out.
The dog ate her voice,
                        another child's logic will say,
and he will be hushed and scolded, sent from the room.

•

Of course we must be readers, be onlookers,
must be delivered
                          to the mother's public scream,
her private no, which begins so viciously
but ends as a whimper, a whisper,
                              a mouthed vacancy.

•

Oh, child, do not listen to that man—
                              he's not your friend,
though he knows about the things you know:
baseball, your mother's beautiful singing voice,
the menu of your Ipod Touch,
                          the constellations.

•

You
      do not know about the things he knows.

•

Onlookers, readers,
                      did you expect the pond would not
be exquisite in morning light,
                          in phrase and cadence slowed
until the wind-stippled surface returned to calm,
the door to the house, in reflection,
                              open.

•

Father,
      your wife will never touch you the same again,
this thing that has happened
                          the only reason she needs,
which, powerless to dispute, you now leave unspoken.

•

Your desire for her was always the root of the problem,
immature boy that you are
                              you must come to terms with
under her cold star-eyes unforgiving, removed.

•

Grow up, grow up, grow up, grow up, grow up!

•

Writer,
        what does your choice of subject matter say about you,
your fears, your view of man's conflict with himself,
your predilections,
                        your lack of understanding your own face?
What do you hope to gain by taking the reader
to the edge of the privet
                              the driver couldn't possibly be expected
to see around, the toddler's excitable, out-of-reach steps?

•

A yard of people all at one time, a chorus,
only a few steps away, shrieking,
reaching,
            squeals of laughter straightway headed toward . . .

•

Do not,
        do not even think about putting your hand there.

•

Child, why would you climb through the culvert?
Who will think to look for you there
                              if you get stuck,

if you panic, if you can't reach the inhaler in your pocket?

•

"Whatsoever things are just, whatsoever things are pure,"
the mother repeats to herself, trying to see
around the edge,
                    "whatsoever things are lovely,
whatsoever things are of good report; if there be any virtue,
and if there be any praise, think on these things,"
but all she can think of
                              is what she thinks on night and day,
following her mind and what it knows,
                                        what it does not know,
what it does not ever ever ever ever want to know
                                        but knows.

•

His friends remember
                        he never passed rumors;
he opened doors like a gentleman, once drew a cello
and called it, jokingly, a self portrait,
was not afraid of spiders,
                        was the first to name all the planets.

•

Meanwhile, the privet hedge needs trimming again,
the pond
        becomes another wide sky's self portrait,
another family moves in, does not know, does not know,
does not
        know why people stare at them in the grocery store.

•

Where is the beginning, where is the end, the mother
will think,
        cupping lotion along extended calves,

as she has done for years, it seems,
to keep the moisture in,
                         to keep from drying out.

                         •

The writer is not, is not, your friend.
Do not go where he, where she,
                         is trying to lead you.
The water will shift, the shore remain distant.
Grow up.
         The trees beyond the pond were never lovely,
only wind-caught, flailing, bending closer, closer,
                                        then snapping back.

                         •

What we know at this time, the sheriff is saying,
is that we're following all leads,
                         and beyond that
he is not willing to speculate, though reporters continue to ask.
The sheriff's face, trying to find the best words,
fills the entire screen,
                         seems to float up out of its depths,
seems to float up out of some deep place he's touched.

                         •

From the beginning,
                         we know the end is coming,
the stars make patterns we trace against the dark,
not one of them can be reached,
                         beneath them
all our words are silence, silenced, none of them
known, not truly,
                         though all we've ever done is speak them,
looking upon them, insane things raised up out of ourselves
we never really trusted the world
                         would not wrench from us,

no, no, never go near that place, don't listen
to any voice but mine,

                  oh, child, why will you not answer?

ANNE BARNGROVER

In Defense of Not Getting Over It, at Least Not for Now

An artist friend told me that her favorite subjects to draw
were those she could not depict all at once: the drunken geometry
of an old house, a majestic pine, our town's river in its lawful
currents—the sky reflected in water the dull-bright colors of money,
but pure. She came back every day to a new vantage point, a new angle,
and that became her blessing and her curse, the way she must return.
The summer I washed dishes to pay a fee, there was one pot I'd wrangle
with for hours—the bane of my evenings, a Herculean feat earned
by its height that reached my knees; its girth, my embrace could not hold.
Someone always burned sauce at the bottom, a thick char that gleamed
despite a soak with dish soap, a dusting of baking soda, a controlled
boil on the stove. There's beauty in it, though: the slow work of dreams
unreached, revision's stench and steam. It's all meant to train one's heart.
I have learned how to build something first by how to take it apart.

ELIZABETH LANGEMAK

The History of Running

The history of running is mostly away,
not chasing but chased, crashing

through darkness. A twig snaps
behind it, stark as a starter's pistol,

and the history of running kicks out
of the blocks and does not turn its head.

The history of running takes place
mostly elsewhere. Like a scream

on a spring day, it seems somehow
source-less, like a dog without tags

plaiting a path around swing sets
and slides, past the whistling track

where high schoolers lope
in disinclined packs. It is never

for sport, and there is no line
a girl could bow her chest over,

arms flung behind her, because
the history of running only ends

in death or more running. While you—
a jogger in shorts sailing over

your thighs like rich ships—
pocket your keys and trot out,

the history of running gets on a bus
and leans its head to the window

until the heat of its breath
makes it too cloudy to see.

ALISON POWELL

Etymology : Heaven

In Hebrew *heaven* is plural
but is often translated
into the singular

One is enough
One can encompass
          the various notions of itself

          self-cleaning
          parthenogenetic
          conveyer
          accountant
          & equinox   & spinning egg

Adam has a word for all—
          even the beasts are given titles—

          & naming being the first form
          & knowing the weight of this

&   feeling himself
          become also
          light and hot as legend

Adam keeps a record

          a list of words
          written in sap
          on animal bellies
          stretched   on a loom
          of bones

until one day

  he rolls them tight as a motive

How sensible

  to take the heaven of first names
  the story of religion which you have begun
  alone
    without helpmeet

  & record it
  on the elastic borderland of the body

See

  how slippery naming
  becomes

  how all living things are godsent
  how all things living will be used

ANAND PRAHLAD

The Platoon

The men of the platoon
         found me different,
         the ones who used
power for bait.

They thought another tune
         with me.
They swelled their cheeks
         with mother's horns

         that blew for miles.
They raised their dicks
with knife blades
         and unrelenting

barrels.
         They stitched their
costumes closed by
         pulling out grenade

pins in rooms with girls
         they sweet talked,
and then laughing.
         They filled their father's

         loins with cigar tips
on girls' skins that
smelled for days.
         And then they sank

their grandfather's boats
       with whispers in my ears
of freckled boys
       in bathroom stalls.

       When they took me,
       when they took all the air
from me, took clippings
of my hair, nails,

my wigs, even torn hose.
       When they pared my skin
and made off
       with the little fat

I worked so hard for,
       with my bones,
they pissed in their grandmother's
       closets.

ADRIAN BLEVINS

Pastoral

My bravery is a daydream that comes from grass I guess
and from the first bio I ever wrote on George Washington Carver
who I chose to forever-love in the third grade
and also to persistently analyze because George was gutsy and brawny
and neurologically-elastic and good at knowing about crop rotation
and mixing things together into a nutritious mash. As a matter of fact
I *did* write about George in longhand in a little diary with a silver key
and though I couldn't spell any of the words like "Tuskegee"
I didn't care and neither did he because we had the mocking birds
to keep us company and not too far away a waterfall we could climb
if we were brave enough, which of course we were. Yes that was
a slippery slope but I loved going to the falls with George
even more than I loved the slick moss and the butter sandwiches
my mom would make with Wonder bread since this was forever ago
and Whole Foods hadn't been incorporated yet
and was as it happens nothing but a series of woebegotten brothers
making molasses on a mountain with a mule and a Granny
who was their mother as well as a stereotype. Yes I have
gone to great lengths to explain myself by way of George to you
and still I feel provoked to continue or maybe just start all over
with a book report on Susan B. Anthony but since that would require
feats of memory and feistiness far beyond me
I'll just assume you've had enough and wander off to the periphery
where all my people live amongst themselves
in an invisible little sachet of thirst-quenching derring-do.

MICHAEL LEVAN

Blue

From the front steps; from the empty streets; / from the kitchen where she rattles pots and pans, / hunting the perfect vessel to slop a can of Spaghettios / and warm them and then ooze them into a bowl, / her spoon scooping every bit of sauce into her mouth, / throat and stomach welcoming home the red's salty warm; / from winter's early-rising moon; from the squeak / and rush of the shower-head turning hot to warm for her, / then lukewarm to frigid for him; / from the loosening bud of her belly; / from the smell of her hair—gardenias again—; / from the CD player that buzzes Morrissey's mannered phrasing, / his warbling yodels; from the finger she used to trace / a line down his cheek to calm him; from the bills in a neat stack on his desk. /

Which is to say it is always there, / and it comes from everywhere. It steals / in and out of the house when he opens the door. / It follows him to the grocery store, tagging along / and begging for his attention like the child / he's yet to have. It disappears with the snow as January's sun / greens the ground below. It is in the dog's bark / that wakes him from dead sleep, the starlings' pre-dawn clicks which remind him he's been awake ever since. /

He steps through the house like a visitor, unsure / where to turn or what to do next. He closes the door, quietly, / and sits on the back deck, bundled warm in his pea coat. / He stares at the blue-black sky like it might answer. / From the window he hears her call his name, / which doesn't sound like his at all, / which makes it easy to say nothing / when she calls him again.

Translation Folio

SHOBA

Translator's Introduction

Paula Gordon

"My father often asks me why I don't write about art in New York, why I insist on boring people to death with descriptions of my childhood and whatnot that anyone can write about. I didn't know how to answer him."

SHOBA WRITES SHORT STORIES ABOUT growing up in Sarajevo in the 1970s and 1980s, his experiences during the 1992–1995 war, and his adventures in the art world. He posts these on his Facebook page for the enjoyment of his 2,300 or so friends and has published dozens of stories and a handful of character studies on his website as an e-book (www.shobaart.com/san-zimskog-ljeta/). "The Test" was first published on Facebook in November 2013, and "The Runner from Džidžikovac" and "Black on White" are from the e-book collection. His stories have also appeared in various Bosnian publications and he writes a column for the Bosnian weekly magazine *Stav* about the vagaries of his present-day life as an artist in New York City—the opening quote comes from his October 11, 2015, column. Shoba's stories in this issue of *Copper Nickel* are the first that have appeared in translation in a U.S. publication.

Shoba started writing in 2004. Otherwise, he is a visual artist—his visual works include paintings, sculptures, installations, and video pieces. He says in the introduction to his e-book, "I took up writing out of desperation, because there was no other means of expression left through which I could describe some important (as well as unimportant) details—things I noticed, characters, events, situations, smells, the atmospheric impressions of specific locations . . . [This book] is just an unambitious attempt to salvage a part of what I experienced and felt, but I hope that many will recognize in it something familiar and even liberating . . ."

I have known Shoba as an acquaintance since the late 1990s—I met him through my work translating art criticism and catalog copy for the Sarajevo Center for Contemporary Art. I ran into his writing in early 2014 via his Facebook posts. When I asked him if I could translate one or two of his stories, he was ambivalent, but he didn't say no. He overcame his reservations after reading an initial draft of "The Test" and has been supportive ever since.

One of the challenges of translating Shoba's stories, especially those set in his grade school years, is replicating the feelings of nostalgia that they evoke in readers who grew up in Sarajevo around the same time. In just a name—a make of car, a corner store, a character in a children's film—Shoba can puncture the veil of time in his readers' minds and invite them to step through into memories of their past. In writing for an American audience, I cannot take advantage of that communal memory; I don't have those shortcuts at my disposal. As a translator, I have to find ways to provide English readers the parts of the picture or the sensations that readers of the original would fill in on their own.

For instance, in "The Test," Shoba refers to the *kecelje* that he and his classmates are wearing. These are long-sleeved smocks, always blue, that elementary school children wore over their street clothes while in school. The point of this in socialist Yugoslavia was to neutralize the class differences between children. For anyone who had to wear one of these growing up, just one word is enough to bring up images and memories of elementary school. For the rest of us, more information is needed. On the other hand, there are commonalities—at least for readers of a certain age: PEZ dispensers, multibarrel multicolored pens, wood-topped metal desks, the sounds of chairs scraping at the end of class. . . . And who among us cannot remember the pangs of test anxiety or the feeling that we don't quite fit in?

The location of the first and third stories is Džidžikovac—a street and a neighborhood in Sarajevo's modern town center. Džidžikovac starts just above the city's main east-west artery and runs diagonally northeast and steeply uphill. It runs alongside a big unruly city park for part of the way, and it is known for a trio of distinctive apartment buildings further up the hill that give the impression of three ocean liners docked up to the street at a 45-degree angle. The apartment complex includes landscaped green space between the buildings, referred to by the residents as the park; this communal open space was and still is a unique and unifying feature of this city neighborhood.

Shoba—in his stories and in his artist persona—embraces the role of naïf and *baksuz*, a Bosnian word that I can explain only by way of Yiddish: a schlemiel. Socially awkward, often in the wrong place at the wrong time, a bumbler. But Shoba's is a bumbler with an inner life. His first-person narrator is deeply self-conscious and introspective and yet has very little self-knowledge. This is especially true in his childhood stories. He notices every visual detail, sound, smell, and sensation and can fall into deep reverie. But when awakened, he reacts instinctively, without thinking. He is easily distracted and follows whatever path or line of thought that presents itself, not looking up or thinking ahead to see where that path might lead.

To the good fortune of his readers, the lack of forethought in this narrator is equaled by Shoba's own clarity of hindsight and his performer's sense of dramatic and comic timing. He tells the stories of the anti-hero, the below-average student, the bumbler, the kid the "good" students look at and wonder, "What was he thinking?" Well, thanks to Shoba's stories, now we know.

The Runner from Džidžikovac

THE WEST TOOK ITS TIME arriving to our Sarajevo neighborhood of Džidžikovac. Sure, there were plenty of Western brand names, all of us had something "Western": Mr. Burić had a Grundig television and Mr. Boras had a Sony; Hamo drove a Mercedes 200D; and Mr. Grin even had the first Pong video game, which he brought back from Canada. Someone might serve a Western dish once in a while, like pizza or hamburgers, but people generally didn't feel it necessary to do anything but go with the flow of established society. The Western way of life was distant—movies were the only way you could see how the West lived. For instance, in almost every American movie at that time you could see someone jogging—running fast for absolutely no reason at all, without being chased. Doing that simply wouldn't occur to us.

And yet, one day there appeared a man in his late thirties who had started to run. He was a real attraction every morning—the old women at their windows watched him and grumbled at how this blond guy, for no reason at all, was disrupting the harmony and natural order of things. People walking on the street would turn, and the postman would laugh out loud and point. Of course the kids taunted him, but he rarely paid us mind.

He always wore a grey cotton sweat suit with some kind of Western phrase written on it in English, and his running shoes were Adidas ROM sneakers, at that time pretty common. After a few laps around Džidžikovac, sweat would start soaking through his grey sweat suit, large stains appearing on his back and chest, increasing the discomfort of those who observed him. The sweat suit had a hood, which the man in question pulled down over his head while he ran, and this intensified the mystery that surrounded this strange runner.

Many waited for the moment when the runner would fall to the pavement and would be picked up by an ambulance or even be picked up by another kind of ambulance, the one from the psychiatric hospital. But no, the runner ran every day, and—day by day—people got used to him.

He didn't have any followers; he was clearly an outlier. Everyone who participated in sports in those days tended to confine their activities to the appropriate location. This runner was a rebel, a veritable Pancho Villa of recreation.

From time to time the runner would be absent for a month or so and no one would know or have any way of knowing where he was. Some would say that he finally went mad, others that he came to his senses and returned to being a normal, calm person. And just when everyone had gotten used to his absence, he would appear again, flying down Džidžikovac Street in a full sprint, leaving everyone with egg on their face.

This went on for a while, until the day it came to a sudden end. One day, two blue-and-white police cars, a Fićo and a Tristać (that is, a Zastava 750 and a Fiat 1300), lights spinning, pulled up to the house where the runner lived. The police filed inside and soon came back out with the runner, and—in full view of the entire neighborhood—put him in handcuffs. Despite his complaints and protestations, they pushed him into the back seat of the Tristać and tore off at full speed down Džidžikovac to the nearest police station.

The first theory to arise was that he was a Western spy who was observing and following the movements of certain persons and that he was working to replace the socialist self-management system with anarchy, an émigré planted to destabilize the social order.

When I rushed inside to deliver the news to my father, he just rolled his eyes. He already knew what had happened. The runner was not jogging for jogging's sake, for his health, or because of a love of the new Western lifestyle that some people were trying to emulate in those days. The reason was, if anything, too simple: When someone steals a German's wallet, then that German runs like crazy after the guy who stole it. Our runner had to be in excellent shape so that he could outrun his victims should any notice him extracting their wallets from their pockets. Mystery solved.

So it turned out that the runner had a reason to jog after all—his larcenous activities required that he be in tip-top shape. And that is how the very idea of jogging as recreation was doomed for a certain period in Džidžikovac. Everyone who decided to run for recreation was declared a potential pickpocket.

Still, times change. Eventually, "running" became respectable, and "runners" were elected to government positions. The occupation of pickpocket was exchanged for the much more profitable occupation of elected official, one that allows you to extract the contents of the wallets of ordinary citizens without the requirement of staying in shape by jogging pointlessly through the streets of Džidžikovac.

The Test

I LOOKED AT THE SHEET of paper on my desk. All those blue lines ready and waiting to guide the orderly and lucid answers I was supposed to write.

I stared through the paper, searching for some unknown point, far beyond the sounds of the classroom—the scritching of pencils being drawn across paper, the groans and scrapes of shifting chairs. The sighs, the whispers. The squeaking of the parquet floor as the teacher paced the room. The rustling of crib sheets being pulled from a multitude of identical school-blue sleeves. And there were other sounds—from the hallway and from the boys' bathroom, where some troublemakers had plugged up a toilet with jelly donuts (filled with artificial jam, our morning snack). The cleaning ladies and Bajro and Slavko, the school maintenance-men/furnace-stokers, were beside themselves.

My thoughts wandered. To familiar neighborhoods, to parks and park-keepers, to playgrounds, to Bajramović and Komšo for cake and ice cream, to the carnival Luna Park that set up summers at the train station, to pilfering PEZ dispensers from the drugstore at the corner of Kralj Tomislav, to shooting blanks from the starter pistol, breaking bottles at the dump, summer vacation at the seaside . . . In short, to everything that might possibly come to mind—except the answers to the test questions.

I held out little hope that I would remember anything that I had (not) heard when I was supposed to be listening. I pictured the thick, heavy, wine-colored ledger (which we all hated regardless of good or bad grades) and the next F that was marching inexorably toward my entry, bringing with it summer school and lectures from my father that would reduce me to the size of an amoeba.

I was already spinning out scenarios of studying for the make-up exam and the long hot summer I would have to spend with some tutor, who, exasperated by my inability to concentrate, would nag me relentlessly while all the other kids played right outside my window. I would go mad because of all the missed cartoons and cowboy movies, the missed games, missed bicycle rides. No picking holly berries and shooting them from homemade blow guns, no knocking around in out-of-the-way corners of Džidžikovac, no snitching fruit from other people's gardens . . .

I opened my pencil case. It was huge—anything and everything you could think of was in there. I took out a pencil sharpener and sharpened the (already sharp) first pencil I grabbed. I used my triangle to gather up the shavings and scrape them over the desk's metal rim into my palm, and then I released them inside the desk, where they joined the gobs of dried chewing gum deposited by generations students who had sat there before me. After I sharpened the pencil, I returned it and the sharpener to their proper place. Then I took out the half-red/half-blue eraser and tested it, rubbing it on the desk. It worked. I began erasing doodles that someone else had left behind. Then I returned the eraser, much dirtier than before, to its place. I pulled out one of my ball-point pens (the all-in-one kind, with six different color inks) and started tracing the creases and seams on the pencil case, making colored circles and ovals in the empty spaces where pencils belonged. Then I pulled out a fountain pen, took it apart and started picking at the ink cartridge. The cartridge was full and my movements were awkward; the ink spilled out onto the new pencil case. I put the fountain pen back together and from the drops of spilled ink, began drawing out spider-web patterns along the surface, all kinds of abstract variations. Next in line was one of my felt-tip pens. I started chewing the cap of the pen, pulling it off. I used the point of my compass to pull out the felt tip. I used the sponge tip, impregnated with ink, to make dots on my blue overshirt. Then I put the pen back together and returned it to its place (but only after chewing on the cap a little more, which at that moment provided a certain amount of satisfaction and relief).

I looked despairingly at the "good" students. Hoping for a miracle, I fantasized that one of them would pass me a scrap of paper containing some beneficial information, a lifeline from this grim reality and the consequences of my feeble study habits and catastrophic lack of attention. I twisted this way and that, trying to catch the eye of someone who might say something, thinking I might notice a dropped crib sheet on the floor or a book under a desk that I could borrow without asking. I watched as classmates sent each other signals, the meaning of which I couldn't begin to guess. Everyone knew that I was a lost cause, that I had nothing to offer in return, and so no one wanted to even look in my direction.

My frustration rose like the suds of a bubble bath under a strong stream of warm water; my panic increasing with each tick of the clock. I wished I could disappear, that the Germans would line me up and shoot me, that an eagle from Mount Romanija would carry me away, that I would be sold to gypsies, that I would be eaten by a fearsome lone wolf, that the evil ogre Bedanec would drag me off to his cave for all time and that his pretty captive Mojca and I would spend the rest of our lives washing pots and pans . . .

And then all at once I remembered something, and I started scribbling on the paper like a madman. Visions from forgotten classes started to rush in, the pen started to give off that familiar inky smell.

And then—the bell rang. Just as I had begun to think I had a chance of accomplishing something, the ship that was ferrying me to the other side of the river started to sink, and sinking along with it was my carefree summer.

A classmate collected all of our papers and put them on the podium in front of the teacher; the hum of students started up like a well-oiled, smooth-running machine, all of them bragging about how well they did. Those of us who were hopeless cases just sat there blinking, dazed, as the others hurriedly stuffed their belongings into their bookbags and jostled out of the room.

I trudged toward the door like I had just peed in my pants, dragging my shabby plastic Marlboro bag with my notebooks, pencil case and black gym shoes behind me.

In my last look back I noticed a tube of tempera paint at the bottom of the classroom aquarium. Someone had just tossed it in there and it was slowly coloring the water red.

The goldfish, which only fifteen minutes before was briskly waving its little fins, slowly turned belly up and floated to the surface of the water, its stomach exposed to the fluorescent lights of that bleak classroom.

Black on White

MAYBE THAT DAY I HAD more luck than usual, and maybe I didn't. It's hard to say. Walking the line between life and death was normal in those days. The war had slowly entered its first winter and now everything was covered with winter's first snow. Džidžikovac had always been idyllic in winter, and it was so even in this evil time. The communal park between our buildings had already started losing its first trees, which were felled to fuel the improvised stoves of the already freezing apartment-dwellers. Occasional distant explosions served to remind us that we could not lower our guard and that danger was always present. Still, one has to live; one has to maintain his sanity however possible. And for that, one needs beer. Lots of beer.

The beer produced by the Sarajevo Brewery in those days still contained a small amount of alcohol, which, when augmented by the men's cologne Pino Silvestre, had the desired effect. The day before, a television and video player were installed in the improvised shelter under the stairs of Rogi's entranceway, and electricity was secured by running an extension cord from the police station next door, which also housed a unit of the Special Tactical Police, whose generator chugged away day and night making electricity, the only electricity in the city.

Pedja and I were carrying a hard-won case of beer, paid for with the very last of our money from selling cigarettes. We were on our way to Rogi's apartment building. The snow was squeaking under our shoes and we picked up the pace. The precious beer was in our hands and both of us were already, silently, nervously, calculating how many beers each of us would drink and who would get the last one, because there was an odd number of us and an even number of beers.

After a few minutes of walking between buildings, we came to a street we had to cross. Džidžikovac Street was fully exposed to Mount Trebević, and bursts of machine-gun fire would from time to time pepper the street. Caution was advised. It had been a foggy day, so we hadn't thought at all about having to run. We had barely taken the first step onto the sidewalk when suddenly the air was sucked out of our lungs . . .

That instant of explosion—it propels you into a state that is neither life nor death, into a strange vacuum, a cosmos, another dimension. Picture and sound disappear, like some kind of orgasm without any enjoyment, a total noncorporeality and nirvana, as if someone turns you off for a second, then turns you on again. At that instant the feeling is not so much panic and fear as much as the instinct of self-preservation, which immediately sends a signal to jump to a safer place—safer being a relative term—than the one you found yourself in when the explosion occurred. Only then comes panic and fear. And after that, deathly silence. And then another shock wave, and the cycle repeats . . .

Pedja and I jumped behind a small wall and threw ourselves to the ground (after nevertheless managing to carefully set down the crate of beer). We could only look at each other in fear, trying to think where we might be safer right then. Definitely on the other side of the street in Rogi's shelter. But we still had to cross Džidžikovac Street, which at that moment was not advisable.

We crouched there for another few seconds in dead silence and then we heard yelling coming from an apartment, through a window covered in plastic sheeting. Someone was wounded and lying in the middle of the street. Pedja and I looked at each other, and out of curiosity rose to peer cautiously over the wall.

On the perfectly white, snow-covered Džidžikovac, a black stain stood out—a giant swath of gunpowder from the exploded mortar shell. And we could just make out, about fifteen meters down from us, in the middle of this black stain, two bodies. The smell of gunpowder and char reached us, bits of gravel and shell fragments were still falling on the powdery snow and on roofs and window ledges.

We didn't know what to do. If we were to go and help those people, another bomb would fall and then we'd be finished too, but we also couldn't just sit there behind the wall looking at people lying there. And then, without either of us making a sign or saying a word, we were running down the street. I braced myself as best I could, hunched over, ducking my head, and surged forward, teeth gritted, waiting for another explosion.

In a few seconds we were beside the victims. I immediately recognized the face of one of them, he was one of the guards who was on the street every day. Next to him was a middle-aged woman who had come to visit someone; the guard was going to accompany her to the reception desk. He showed some signs of life—he was writhing and struggling to breathe. The woman lay there lifeless. Her fur coat was totally shot through with shrapnel, and pieces of fur and flesh were scattered everywhere around. I put a finger on her neck and pressed down on her main artery. There was no pulse.

I turned and looked at Pedja, who had already started to unzip the guard's black jacket. Something was sticking and we had to tug a little at the zipper. The jacket opened up and immediately revealed his intestines, which popped and peeked out of a hole in his black sweater like small pink balloons. He was gasping for breath in a death rattle but we told him that everything would be alright, not to worry about anything, someone had already called an ambulance. A car arrived almost that very moment, and we grabbed him and shoved him into the back seat. The driver stepped on the gas and the car sped down the street toward the hospital.

I can't remember what movie we watched; I washed down the beers faster than usual. We were trying to purge what couldn't be washed away—the bitter taste of impotence and disbelief. The dried blood was still on our sleeves, the smell of charred remains and death filled our nostrils. The hell that had found us had no intention of leaving; instead, it dragged us deeper and deeper into an abomination and horror beyond human imagination. We asked ourselves why this was happening to us, why we of all people had to be there at that moment to see with our own eyes how life exits a human body.

And finally, it could have been us lying there lifeless on the street. If the gunner on the other side, after downing a liter of cheap brandy, had just a little more nervously or eagerly rotated the frozen, rusty wheel of the mortar launcher's aiming mechanism so the barrel was just a little higher . . . if the gunpowder had been just a little drier . . . if the wind had blown from the opposite direction . . . maybe the situation would have been different and the guard and the woman in the fur coat would have been the ones horrified to witness the death of two young men, who, instead of watching a film in a makeshift shelter powered by stolen electricity, would be lying next to a shattered wooden crate, spilled beer mixing with their warm blood.

Translated from the Bosnian by Paula Gordon

EVELYN SOMERS

King of the Big Ticket

CALL THE PROTAGONIST ALEX Y., to protect identity. And call the spouse Casey Q. And there was Lex. All three names might be gender-neutral.

Alex is either the husband or the wife. Ditto Casey. Perhaps they were a same-sex couple. Lex, the alter, may not have been the same gender as Alex; but how would Alex even have known, if Alex was unaware at first that Lex existed: How does your left hand know what your right hand is doing?

And what is gender, anyway?

Answer #1: a hand doesn't have a head, so it doesn't know anything. Even muscle-memory doesn't "belong" to a hand; it belongs to the brain that makes the hand write things it will never be capable of understanding.

Answer #2: gender is a construct. It is only one way of separating everyone in the world into two groups of billions of people. There are other ways to do it. We would all like to have authority to decide the categorizing principle. Natural selfishness would make us draw the line to put ourselves on the more advantaged side. We would all like to be King of the Big Ticket. But of course, for all of us living now, the line was drawn, the ticket awarded, before we existed.

Alex Y. was a thin child with white skin and deep-set, riveting eyes, but as a baby Alex was blubbery like a pocket Buddha. S/he looked like the creation of a balloon-animal artist, with flesh rolls you ought to be able to pop.

Alex, like the Pillsbury Dough Boy, was an invitation to poke and squeeze. There used to be a photograph on Alex and Casey's bedroom wall of the black-girl help from Alex's childhood, Scharalotte, cradling the fat pale child against her young bosom, her brown hand clasped around a plump leg. In the picture, Scharalotte's nail-bitten fingers pressed into Alex's abundant flesh, though not enough to hurt: Alex was smiling, round cheeks puffing up to almost conceal the dark, magnetic, semirecessed eyes.

Scharalotte was not illiterate, fyi. She was not a natural nurturer of white babies. No such thing: she was a brilliant seventeen-year-old scholarship girl who from the age of twelve had determined that she would commit her life to studying endangered languages. She was a freshman linguistics/math double major at an esteemed university and the mentee of a Canadian friend of Alex's parents—who were going bonkers because Alex wasn't taking to the sweeter, duller sitters usually available, the ones with cute clothes and manicures. So they'd cast wide a desperate conversational net and phoned and asked everyone if they knew any razor-sharp young woman or man who would sit Alex—someone equally, or even more, gifted, whose intellect oozed from their pores and would comfort Alex and make Alex feel safe, among friends.

Because a smart baby senses early on that stupidity is out to get it.

Scharalotte was who they caught in the net.

But in the photograph, is Scharalotte holding Alex? Or Lex? Casey, the spouse, would like to know this: Was there a Lex from the beginning, or did Lex come later, when Scharalotte left, as a companion for Alex in Alex's loneliness?

Because to be very smart is to be have your pool of potential friends reduced to a scant handful—there are so few like you. Casey knows this, and sometimes it makes Casey sad unto death. People don't get people like Alex. Specifically, they don't comprehend the unspeakable, chronic loneliness of the hyperconscious self.

There are old home movies of Alex as a child. Casey has watched them in search of an explanation for the things Alex does sometimes that violate convention and Casey's expectations of what a spousal covenant means. Such as the dry, sarcastic cuts on Casey that Lex makes in public; they just flow out, unfiltered; often they're directed at Casey's museum work. *Lex* is an asshole. But there's a lot more to it than that, and, curiously, *Alex* is sensitive—rarely critical of anyone.

And another thing Casey tries to understand by watching the movies: Alex's long-term affair with a woman almost twenty years older, which Alex insists was a confected fantasy or tries to blame on Lex. Casey understands that it was Lex, but Casey knows Alex had a part in it.

Or Alex's frequent ghost dreams, in which s/he begins to thrash and moan. For Alex, nightmares are a common occurrence, but the ghost dreams are unique in that they wake Casey every time, where the other dreams play quietly in Alex's head, not disturbing Alex's body. Under the spell of a ghost dream, Alex will begin to undulate in the soft green sheets, and then to thrash, arms and legs flying out unpredictably and hitting Casey in the chest and other places. Next Alex begins to make a low, ghostly sound, half teakettle-whistle, half moan: Ooooowooooooowoooo. It starts inaudibly, quite low in pitch and volume, and quickly rises. Casey has to shake Alex hard or roll Alex over to stop the whistling and thrashing. Then Alex wakes, relieved to be rescued—quivering, scared—and tells Casey about the dream. There's always a haunted house in it, an ancient lake, deep woods, a ghost chasing Alex. Ghosts, plural, sometimes. The intent of the ghosts is perpetually ambiguous. Of course: spirits are the poetic fungi on the protoessential self. Why should they state their purpose in easy signage? Casey wonders each time: Who was dreaming? Lex? Or Alex?

Casey wonders, too, whether the ghost in the dream is the other half of hir spouse who was dreaming. It's all too confusing. But the nightmares seem vaguer and more psychologically loaded; they're about something larger.

When Alex was seven or eight, Alex had a friend a few years older named Howie Rollie. Everyone called him "Howlie." What brought Howlie and Alex together was their common psychic pain, visible to those who didn't share it by their odd physiques and demeanors. Alex was tall, gangly, pasty white as printer paper, with big bones and prominent veins that showed blue through Alex's handsome, puppy-like legs and feet. Howlie was wiry, with unnervingly wide-set eyes. If you wanted to cast a gang member in a budget film, you might cast an adult Howlie: little and incredibly muscled, with those eyes that ought almost to be on stalks, they were so far apart.

One movie Casey has watched is of a birthday party, Howlie's, that was held at a local park. Howlie's bald policeman uncle barbecued hot dogs, and his cute but jittery mom (a widow) dipped ice cream with stringy brown arms from a barrel-looking extra-large ice cream freezer that was ahead of its time in speed, coldness, and the creaminess of the ice cream it made. Alex still remembers the ice cream, which had cubes of gold-colored fresh peaches in it. Scharalotte, in her twenties then, took the footage—she was a graduate student, dissertating, holing up in the library stacks in a cage with her books and cassettes; the cage walls were covered with grafitti over grafitti, like a palimpsest, from decades of frustrated students. The language could have been a dissertation in itself. Her favorite? *Jack Bob ducks socks don't Trust his Ass* in green marker with a terrifying darkened smiley after "Ass" instead of a period: ☻ She was still in the lives of Alex's parents, then, still working for them when she wasn't writing, helping with Alex. She tutored Alex in calculus, and they drilled together on medieval French literature and psycholinguistics because Alex was so far ahead of the class in all subjects that additional intellectual stimulation was critical for keeping Alex from disintegrating into a puddle of crazed loneliness. You think Alex is a boy, right? Because Alex is so smart and I said "puppy-like" about the feet.

Howie Rollie would be institutionalized for mental illness in his twenties. His mind simply splintered from everything in it that had been stabbing knives in his psyche for years, and his nervous mother, who'd really loved him, would be left with the kind of pathetic, inadequate mementos that a child mentally unstable from the beginning leaves when it finally crosses into madness: the words *Mene, mene, tekel, parsin* inscribed everywhere—on the backs of receipts and the front covers of phone books. On the underside of a medicine-cabinet shelf, with some pieces of hardened green gum, and even carved into the hardwood bedroom floor beside her bed. Also, a Mother's Day card in which he'd drawn himself and his mother standing together by some unusually tall flowers, with x's over their eyes, possibly to indicate that they were dead.

The birthday-picnic footage that Casey has watched begins with a bizarre relay in a park with rolling hills and tidy shelters, on a mild June day. Alex was prone to wildness because of being so readily bored. Alex was especially wild in social situations; anxiety spiked then because Alex was hypersensitive to the fact that everyone else knew how they were supposed to act, and Alex did not. Howlie was wild for a different reason: he was becoming insane. The backstory that preceded the relay is that Howlie's uncle, an earnest police captain, committed to being a manly role model, loved his sister and realized after Howlie's father was electrocuted that Howlie was going to need a man to guide him. He was trying to oblige. But he was single and bad with animals and children. Grilling hot dogs for a dozen or so strange kids (because Howlie's friends were all weirdo-nerds) had tested his nerves. The kids made so much noise! They kept trying to help, or to steal half-cooked hot dogs off the grill—he wasn't sure which—so he gave them two packages of raw hot dogs and two long, extra barbecue forks that Howlie's mom had brought and told them to organize a game in which they divided the hot dogs into two piles and formed equal lines at a distance of about twelve yards. He didn't really suppose this activity would hone any skills, but they'd get some exercise and stay off his back. The kid at the head of each line would run with the fork to the pile opposite, spear a hot dog and run back, holding the fork ahead. The next kid would grab the hot dog off the tines and pass it down the line, then take the fork and run back to the pile. The person at the back of the line was required to dispose of the hot dog somehow, but Howlie's uncle had not given any directions as to how. Some of the kids ate the raw wieners. One girl buried hers in a shallow grave. Most of them tore up the hot dogs and flung them away, into the Tiger Tot Lot, a fenced area with a jungle theme and play equipment for the littlest park users. Soon the toddler play area was littered with rubbery, red pieces of flesh.

The movie of this game is upsetting to watch. Kids are running at each other hard, wielding forks with long, sharp tines. They're screaming and jumping and ripping up and throwing hot dogs and trying to stuff them in each other's mouths. When the piles of hot dogs are exhausted, the two kids with the forks—one of them is Howlie, the other unidentified—run around threatening other kids. Finally, Howlie wrests the second fork from the other kid and leaps onto a picnic table, brandishing both. Alex hesitates. The film shows Alex trying to decide. There must be a protocol, but Alex doesn't know what it is. Jump up on the table with Howlie? When Casey (Is Casey the husband? The wife?) watches the video, s/he immediately recognizes a classic right-brain/left-brain conflict. Half of Alex is Dionysian response, wanting to leap onto the table, seize the moment and participate in Howlie's freestyle performance. The other half is frantically calculating the social equation, without understanding the value of x: If I jump up on the table, will I be empowered by the height and the long, sharp fork? Or will I be demoted to an object of ridicule because it's Howlie, and he's always out of whack?

Alex's eyes gleam, weighing things. There's a strange light in them that gives Casey a shiver. The gleam angers Casey because Casey suspects it's how Alex looked in the bedroom of Mrs. Logan's house, the moment before Lex launched into unrepentant adultery. Casey also suspects the moment of decision—the gleam—may indicate a first imperceptible fissure in Alex's self.

In the movie, Alex goes for the table. It only takes a second for the gleam to fade, a step to be taken. A leap. Alex is up there. You can see Alex's exultation when s/he realizes it was the right choice. All the other kids circle around the table. Howlie is shouting; he hands one of the forks to Alex. Alex starts shouting, too. It's remarkable that during the most horrifying moments of this sequence, the camera never wavers. Scharalotte never put it down to try to stop anyone from hurting anyone else. She was too interested to stop. And the camera always mediates, buffers. The kids continue to chant. Alex and Howlie are visibly out of control—what might they do? Stab each other? Leap from the table and start spearing the shouting kids the way, a few minutes ago, they were all spearing hot dogs? There's no sound, but they were all shouting Howlie's trademark phrase: *Mene! Mene! Tekel! Parsin!*

ASSUMPTIONS ABOUT GENDER ARE LIKE the birthmark of Hawthorne's story: indelible. Fatal. Alex is male? I think so? Maybe. You think so. Because Alex's most intimate friendship is with a boy, Howlie, and that kind of total friendship between the two sexes is rare, maybe impossible. Because Scharalotte, a young woman, has formed a nurturing bond with Alex, and women nurture men, not their own sex. Because people sometimes think Alex is an asshole. Because extreme behavior is expected in boys, but in a girl it's an unseemly surprise. Because Casey tries to understand Alex—and that's a wife thing, right? Because Alex sometimes curses, and Casey and Scharalotte are rarely heard to. Because you might let your young son hang out with a boy who was a little on the edge, like Howlie. But not your daughter. Because Alex grabs a barbecue fork and jumps on the picnic table and gets crazy and screams, just a tick away from stabbing someone.

Scharalotte nannied and tutored Alex until she finished her Masters in mathematics and her doctorate in Language Endangerment and Revitalization. Brilliant as she was, she might have migrated to another institution in another state and received a more generous fellowship if she'd been willing to leave Alex. But she loved Alex, who was, if not her soulmate, her almost equal in intelligence. If Alex was always comforted in the aura of her intoxicated brainpower, Scharalotte found in Alex adoring acceptance and a mirror that reflected her most acute but fleeting insights back to her and helped her to concretize the flow of her thoughts. Think about how much mental gold dust is washed away by the river of distraction because no one ever panned it out. Alex was Scharalotte's pan.

She'd gotten very lucky that her intellect was recognized and rewarded. She'd had an underprivileged upbringing: raised by her grandmother, a hard-working black-skinned lady named Mrs. Logan, whose indulgence was her CareFree Curl hairstyle (which she kept defined, shiny and moist with daily applications of the Curl

Activator). Mrs. Logan liked Wednesday night Bible study and a shot of bourbon twice a week. Also, she liked giving Scharalotte what advantages she could afford to. In childhood Mrs. Logan had been an exceptional student at her negro school, surprising many teachers (also black) who expected her to be slow because she was so poor and smelled bad—there was no indoor plumbing, not much soap. She'd hoped to attend a business college for young women after she graduated high school—the first in her family to do so, the only one besides Scharalotte, decades later—but her parents just laughed at her. With what money? And who would let a colored girl into their school? In 1931? So she cleaned houses for Scharalotte's education and made sure her granddaughter's college and then graduate work was prayed about at every church function. Scharalotte had grown up in the church (AME), and when she held the camera on Howlie and Alex and heard them shouting "Mene, mene, tekel, parsin," she recognized that it wasn't gobbledygook: they were shouting the words that the disembodied hand in the Book of Daniel wrote on the plaster when King Belshazzar's pagan guests drank from the goblets that his father, Nebuchadnezzar, had seized as plunder from Jerusalem's temple.

Howlie's chanting of the ancient Hebrew words was not the pressurized speech of mania. It was his personal brain worm, implanted in him by a string that had come down from the ceiling one night and touched his head while he was asleep. It was the night after he'd played Daniel in a Sunday school skit. He woke, and saw the string on his forehead, and went back to sleep. After that, the words never left.

He felt happy every time he sang his encrypted song of praise to the only man he really remembered being nice to him, Dr. Frank Clay. From the time he was four, Howlie had walked to the nearby Baptist church every Sunday with his mother. There he played by himself in the nursery and later attended Dr. Clay's elementary Sunday school class. After his father died, he walked to church every Sunday alone because his mother was mad at God's intransigence regarding death (she thought He should have resurrected Howlie's father after the accident). Dr. Clay found Howlie stressful, but he was a compassionate man. One winter, for four weeks the class studied the book of Daniel. Dr. Clay prepared a lesson on Daniel's interpreting skills: the class would perform a skit.

Dr. Clay was the hand. To practice, at home he set up a small chalkboard in the living room and ducked down behind the coffee table. In this uncomfortable position, without looking, he raised his arm sideways and wrote in hot-pink chalk the ancient Hebrew characters. *Mene, mene, tekel, parsin:* מנא מנא תקל ופרסין. His wife came in and watched him. People thought doctors were omniscient, disengaged from dailiness. But here was Frank, after a grueling day in clinic and then being called back for an emergency consult, on the floor with his nose in the carpet, trying to write upside down and backward, practicing so he could fulfill the expectations of a class of grade-school children. He was a good person, not remote at all, just shy, not perfect but unusually decent, and she understood why sometimes strangers came up to her and wanted to talk about how he'd saved their lives.

That Sunday (Howlie was seven), Dr. Clay gave Howlie the part of Daniel. He wanted Howlie to feel valued. The children opened their Bibles to the story and looked at the picture, in which Daniel was being ceremonially dressed with a necklace and robe (for interpreting), and the hand, behind him, was writing *Mene* on a vignetted rectangle of blond plaster.

The skit proceeded. The children drank from Styrofoam cups decorated like goblets and pretended they were King Belshazzar's party, praising the pagan gods.

Dr. Clay crouched below the table, put up his hand and wrote the characters, and as the hand popped out, the children shrieked a scripted shriek. *Mene, mene, tekel, upharsin*, wrote the hand.

The child-Belshazzar demanded that Howlie (Daniel) translate the words. Howlie complied. He had a good memory and recited the scripture verbatim. For deciphering the characters that predicted Babylon's impending overthrow, Howlie was decorated with a gold chain and proclaimed the third-highest ruler of the kingdom. Belshazzar put the necklace on him; Mrs. Clay had loaned it.

"You are the third-highest ruler," announced Belshazzar-kid.

"Of what?" asked Howlie.

Belshazzar looked at the illustration in his Bible of the vignetted rectangle of plaster. It looked like a ticket. He didn't know king of what. "You're the King of the Big Ticket," said Belshazzar, pointing at the picture.

"Oh, okay," said Howlie.

BUT THEN SHE LEFT.

It was the bleakest day of Alex's life. Bleaker, even than the day years later when Alex married Casey.

The day of their wedding, Alex threw up twice. Alex choked out the vows and would not do the mutual cake-feeding for fear of vomiting again. Alex expected Scharalotte to appear at the back of the chapel and and shout Alex's name, like Dustin Hoffman. Alex imagined riding away on a bus with Scharalotte, to tribal cultures. But instead, Alex had married Casey. Alex needed Casey in multiple ways; Casey cared for Alex, and the two had been sexually magnetized to one another from the moment of their meeting. Casey was smart, competent, sensitive, and had a body that sang to Alex's body. But there was a Scharalotte-shaped hole inside Alex.

Their wedding was years after Scharalotte left, but Alex had never forgotten Scharalotte's departure. The night before, Alex's parents and Mrs. Logan and the two young people—one ten, one twenty-six, had gone out to dinner at a family-style buffet. The conversation was halting and uncomfortable, but Mrs. Logan felt the power of the Holy Ghost beating back her anxiety. They ate, and as they got ready to leave, she laid a hand on Alex's hair, and felt a shock go through her.

She had felt this once before, in her impoverished prepubescence. There had been a tomboyish girl who lived in a Quonset building near the school; she'd had a crush on smart and gentle Mrs. Logan. She threw dirt at the girl Mrs. Logan had been, and when Mrs. Logan was walking to school, the little dark Tomboy followed her down their chuckholed street with no sidewalks. Stalked her. The Tomboy was not a "normal" girl; she was angry and violent, and though Mrs. Logan tried to ignore her without doing so obviously (because Mrs. Logan was kind from her earliest years), there were times when she couldn't. Once the Tomboy appeared out of nowhere while Mrs. Logan was running to the store for her mother to get some lard. The Tomboy had a bag of taffy and offered one like bait. Mrs. Logan carried this image in the personal photo album in her brain, of the Tomboy holding out a red-and-white swirled piece of wrapped taffy. There was the dark hand, thin (no one had been fat, back in the '20s, that she remembered). Dirt in the nails and the dry, cracked knuckles, a little dirt on the twisted, translucent paper. There was the irregular nugget-shaped offering of lesbian love too young to even understand that that's what it is.

She took and ate the taffy because she couldn't not—she had seen the scars on the Tomboy's arm. This picture in her brain: the burn-scarred arm, the dirty hand, the pink peppermint candy. And when she touched the Tomboy's hand, she felt the doubleness, the split, that she would feel again as an elderly woman, touching Alex's hair in the family steakhouse the night before Scharalotte left.

Scharalotte drove away the next morning in a rusty yellow Datsun B210 with some age on it. She came to say good-bye to Alex, but Alex picked up the wrapped present she'd brought, a pair of books by Iris Murdoch and Noam Chomsky, and heaved it over the side of the deck, where the Ys had all been eating breakfast.

Scharalotte said Alex's name and left.

"I'll miss you" in her voice.

After a minute, Alex followed. The adult Ys let Alex go, imagining the two needed privacy. Alex's mother sat eating her child's pain. It looked like fruit to Mr. Y, who reflected that loss is endemic to life and was sad, nevertheless, that Alex's heart had to be broken. You think Alex is a girl because Alex's father saw it this way: as a "heartbreak," requiring tender sympathy for the broken one. Are you wallowing in a sexist rut? Walk away from the shabby-chic dining table with bowls of fresh pineapple, the two parents like miles-apart points on this infinite line of story-time. Come through a big room piled with old picture frames and drum parts, and the bright galley kitchen. In the front yard are spreading, bug-chewed, waxy-leaved hostas. It's July, and the hydrangea blooms are dried, brown drooping fists of flower death. A mud-dauber drones around its beige plaster domicile. Its legs are miraculously agile yet precisely puppet-like, as if God's strings were maneuvering it. Which they are. The Datsun is chugging away, out of sight. Scharalotte is a genius driving toward her illustrious future. Alex, in the grass, is rolling slowly back and forth, moaning a dirge. *No, no, no, no, no. No, no. NO.* Whether or not there was already a crack, a division, dating from Howlie's birthday picnic, now there is a total split. Trauma, caused by Scharalotte leaving, provoked Alex to dissociate completely for the first time, as proved by things Lex wrote during this period of grieving, scattered bits of paper around the Ys' house marked by irreal thoughts and dramatic changes in handwriting and a writing voice that alternated between the whine of a little child and a wordy pedantry that was never how Alex spoke or wrote.

•

LTCS Dissertation of the Year Award Winner: Scharalotte Logan (PhD '84)

Title: Excitement = Wordiness: Lexical Impoverishment and Periphrasis among Speakers in a State of Transgressive Excitement

Chair: Dr. Ydel Erutsio

Q: Tell us about the genesis of the idea for your award-winning dissertation?

Scharalotte Logan: As an undergraduate, I was videotaping a children's birthday party at a park, and the children were playing a wild game with hot dogs that ended in threats of violence and a clear attempt by two of the children to establish their power over the others. I was struck by how, in an excited state, they "lost" lexical items that I believed they knew but had not yet mastered. I have an eidetic memory, but for documentation I kept a tally in the dirt with the toe of my shoe, of instances in which they substituted an imprecise periphrastic structure for a more precise but morphosyntactically complex expression. I didn't know at the time that it would result in a dissertation—my original research was about acquisition of iambic stress patterns. But the grafitti above my desk in the stacks at the library also revealed that transgressive writing, when it's hurried and produced in a state of excitement, may exhibit a similar periphrasis. So I started to be fascinated, and I changed my subject.

Logan, Scharalotte. When Words Disappear: A Case Study of Two Cultures. Chicago. City Press, 1989. 284 pp.

On the surface Logan's book narrates the cultural impact of a vanishing dialect distinct enough to be termed a language. But despite the modest title, Logan has bigger aims, and by the end has waded fearlessly into the Fodorian territory of mentalese and the modularity of the mind . . . This is a provocative work of scholarship by a linguist who appears more than a little interested in pioneering a philosophical approach to the dire subject of language extinction.

THE DAY SCHARALOTTE LEFT, ALEX became two people. *Lex* never got over Scharalotte. Lex was in ways quite infantile. *Alex* went on to live a life. After rolling around in the grass awhile, Alex looked up and saw Mrs. Y standing there with the books Scharalotte had brought. "Why don't you read these?" she said.

The margins of these books were where Lex expressed sometimes, early in the morning or late at night, while Alex went on about the usual business of growing up, going to college, graduate school in microengineering, meeting other like-minded and abled people for social/sexual outlets, moving out of the Ys' home, landing an internship with a well-known toy company, executing strategic moves, discerning that marriage was a logical next step and moving in with Casey. Marrying Casey. Waiting for Scharalotte.

CASEY AND ALEX HAD BEEN married five years when Scharalotte returned. There were no children yet, though they talked about wanting two, to prevent the loneliness of their children being alone. Alex logged long, less creative hours than you might imagine: toy development was hostage to vapid celebrity-worship. It was hobbled by safety standards of the ASTM and CPSC. Alex's creations were in bondage to a capricious, profane and litigious early twenty-first-century culture. It was 2003.

Casey was a museum curator, with days that were more pleasant. Casey scheduled and hung exhibits. Casey jogged at lunch. Casey explained the ceramic spoons of ancient Eastern households to the kind of children that had never quite understood Alex. Casey was fearless, wiping dust out of a two-thousand-year-old urn with a puffy bottle-brush tool; and neither was Casey awed by rare antiquities. S/he gazed every day on the beauty manufactured by millenia of the anonymous dead and thought about it like this: it was all just a lot of stuff that got left behind.

On their free weekends Casey and Alex liked float trips. They camped and made love in their tent. Their bodies were still magnets for each other. Alex's chest drove Casey wild. Were there breasts on it? You decide. Casey brought cream-filled donuts for breakfast, with gridded outsides dusted with powdered sugar. Alex brought a book or two, and in the night Lex wrote in them by flashlight sometimes, and the next morning Alex would be exhausted; the day would start slowly, and they'd only hike a fraction of the distance they'd planned.

Mrs. Logan was ninety now. Her mind operated by fluid impressions and memories that slid back and forth like wooden beads along the string of the years of her life. She was fit and vigorous for her age, though; she entered a 5K race for senior citizens and won in her age class but could not remember afterward where she lived. Police and social services had to be called, and Scharalotte came back to put her in an assisted living facility, Woodpecker Hill. It was the same place where Howlie Rollie had been living for years, where Alex visited Howlie and talked over toy ideas and God and Dr. Frank Clay with the old friend. Howlie loved it when Alex visited. He felt valued when Alex asked him his opinions about toys. He had a laminated sign on his door that said **King of the Big Ticket**. That was what he'd called himself, first jokingly and later seriously, ever since the play in Sunday school. Though Alex always called him "Howie" for the sake of Howlie's broken mind. One Friday afternoon, leaving Howlie's room, Alex shut the door softly and turned the corner. And it was Scharalotte, twenty years older.

THEIR AFFAIR STARTED IMMEDIATELY, THAT same afternoon. Alex left the car in the parking lot at Woodpecker Hill and rode in Scharalotte's rental compact to Mrs. Logan's house. Alex was thirty; Scharalotte was forty-six. The years rolled back, and they talked about what they'd lost, breaking apart. Alex: a soul companion. Scharalotte: a mirror of her mind. Alex nestled under Scharalotte's arm, but it was really Lex, nestling like a child: Lex in the car with her; Lex walking, distressed, a little fogged, into the blue shotgun home in the poor neighborhood Mrs. Logan had never left, with the La-Z-Boy Scharalotte had bought her grandmother. The pretty blue Persian rug, and other nice, new things from Scharalotte. But the kitchen smelled like biscuits and gravy; it was antique because Mrs. Logan would only cook with the dented steel bowls and humble pans she'd always used. There was a garage-sale plastic decoration in the shape of a tiny skillet, with a prayer, over her stained, scratched-up sink:

Lord, bless this homely kitchen
Where we cook and pray and eat
And help us know that here on Earth
We are Thy hands and feet

In the bedroom, they knew but ignored that it was adultery. Sex was facilitated by the fact that Scharalotte had never married and was in between relationships.

Scharalotte was on sabbatical and had flown in from a village in Tete province, northern Mozambique, where she was engrossed in rigorous fieldwork, to take care of Mrs. Logan. She was going back soon; but only three months remained of her leave, and then she'd be home. "Home" was halfway across the country—but that was why God had made airplanes, she told Alex. She said it jokingly, and Lex laughed, though they both believed it was fate: their reunion, this unlooked-for consummation. Casey knows the facts now and knows they thought this. It angers hir because Alex—Lex—made a conscious decision to put the past (Scharalotte) before the present (Casey). Casey's museum work has convinced Casey that the past is not worth the paper it's recorded on. The past is like a snake's skin. You have to shed it or else, trapped in an ever-tightening wrapper, you will die.

The affair went on for four years, until Scharalotte was fifty and Alex thirty-five. Then two things happened to end it: 1) Casey found out; 2) Scharalotte was having dinner with Mrs. Logan one evening in the dining room at Woodpecker Hill, when the Tomboy sat down next to Mrs. Logan. Mrs. Logan had not seen the Tomboy in over seventy years because the Tomboy had died of diphtheria at fifteen. The Tomboy was only fifteen still; she had not aged. She stroked Mrs. Logan's arm and said she, the Tomboy, hadn't ever stopped loving Mrs. Logan, and then she whispered in Mrs. Logan's ear, "Look. You're surrounded by fools and liars. It's been that way all your life. Do you have one true friend with a heart like yours?" She whispered that Scharalotte had been profaning Mrs. Logan's home with a young white person. Mrs. Logan listened and ate her soup. A food-service person breezed by, and Mrs. Logan called for another bowl for her old friend.

Scharalotte looked at her sharply: there was no old friend that she could see.

Mrs. Logan gazed back across the table at her granddaughter. "You're a whore," she said. "Give me my key." Old though she was, she felt seared by betrayal. She would have thrown her soup on Scharalotte, if she'd been sure of her aim, if age hadn't made her so shaky.

The Tomboy got up and left.

"I'm sorry," said Scharalotte. After a while she left, too, without giving her grandmother the house key, and Mrs. Logan sat wondering what her life had added up to: potential never realized because she'd been poor, black and female decades before the Civil Rights movement; years of hard work and trying to be Christ's hands and feet; a common-law "marriage" that was among her worst memories, which had produced a worthless daughter—Mrs. Logan didn't even know where she was. A granddaughter she'd adored, now transformed into a slut. She remembered what it had felt like when she'd laid her hand on Alex's head at the steak house. She'd seen the trouble coming, but it had been a pinpoint far in the future, and you can put the thumb of your mind over the speck of a distant problem in motion and hide it, deny its relentless approach.

Scharalotte and Lex met one last time, at Mrs. Logan's house. They didn't have sex. They cleaned the house together; they washed the sheets in which they'd desecrated everything. Scharalotte baked a peach pie—she was a good cook; she'd learned from her grandmother—and took it to a Vietnamese family across the side street, introducing herself in their own language, to their amazement: an unknown black woman with a pie just shows up at your door speaking Vietnamese.

Scharalotte and Lex put out pansies and geraniums on Mrs. Logan's front porch. Then they drove to Woodpecker Hill and together recounted their penance to Scharalotte's grandmother, who received them coolly and said she would consider what to do about the house. She would let Scharalotte know her plan, after she had consulted an old friend of hers.

The Tomboy never returned while Mrs. Logan was alive, but on the morning Mrs. Logan died in her sleep, the Tomboy was there to take her hand as she crossed over.

SCHARALOTTE CONTINUES TO TEACH AND do scholarship; she travels, does fieldwork, writes magnificent, ground-breaking books. She hasn't married, and is celibate most of the time.

After Mrs. Logan died, Howlie was moved to Mrs. Logan's old room. No one knows why. There's an androgynous teenaged black girl who visits him sometimes. She's rough and dirty. But she always speaks the truth. Howlie's mother almost never comes; it hurts too much and leaves her depressed. But Alex still visits faithfully, and now the black girl, who sometimes gives Howlie candy.

Casey and Alex blunder on. Their bodies were always made for each other.

The toy business goes unpredictably, opening out or folding back year to year, like an accordion. Kids change and don't. Toys evolve and regress. Laws block the best of Alex's ideas.

The museum is a sanitized way for Casey to hate the past. Specifically, for Casey to hate what Lex and Scharalotte did.

Lex has mostly disappeared, but Casey still has questions.

Every weekday at the museum, when Casey takes a lunch break, s/he walks purposefully from the cool exhibit area to the claustrophobic office. Lunch is half a bagel and a cup of blue yogurt. You assume female, because Casey eats yogurt. Really?

Rarely, Casey eats after the jog. Eat and run—not run and eat.

Running, Casey thinks about how hard it has been, being with Alex. Brilliance is its own society, and Casey will always come second.

Casey's jogging route goes past a boutique where two gay men sell leather clothes and spiky jewelry. Passing it, Casey's thoughts usually go to sex and gender. If Casey were reading this story, s/he would tell you that whatever opinions you've formed about the gender of the characters are wrong. The characters have no gender. They aren't people; they are names, words. Words, words, words, words. Casey: a word. Scharalotte: a word. The Ys. Mrs. Logan. Poor, poor Howlie and his mother, and the Tomboy and everyone else.

Every day, Casey returns to the museum and changes from a jogging person trying to recover from hurt back into a curator. There is a line in you, and if you stand on one side of it, you are King of the Big Ticket; and if you stand on the other side, you are nobody much.

As Casey was changing back into professional garb today, this is what Casey was thinking: *Lex is not a person. Lex is Lex. A word. Alex: a word that has Lex in it. We're all lives made of words, with other words in them. We're all a brain split in half. All* not *man and* not *woman.*

The Tomboy, sitting cross-legged on the floor in cutoff shorts and green Converses, was giving these ideas to Casey, and though Casey couldn't hear the Tomboy speaking, Casey's brain received it all.

IN THE EVENINGS, AT HOME, Casey loves but doesn't know whom anymore. It's not Alex or Lex; it's not their daschund, Britomart. Casey's been drinking a little, until s/he figures it out. It might be Frank Clay, Howlie's Sunday school teacher, whom Casey heard about once but has never met. A good, kind man. It might be God, who makes walk the wasps with exquisite puppetry. It might be the spirit of Howlie, the poetic fungus on Casey's protoessential self. Casey saw his hand one night, in hir own version of one of Alex's ghost dreams.

Howlie's hand came out of the wall above Casey's head. It wrote and wrote and wrote and wrote and wrote. *Mene, mene, tekel, parsin,* it wrote.

It wrote: *They call me King of the Big Ticket.*

It wrote: *You think I'm a girl.*

It wrote: *But I'm not.*

URSULA BROOKS

No Human Power

•

AT THE HOUSE, I BUILD and watch the fire. Fire's a terrible way to go.

At the house, the man keeps dead animals everywhere. The coyote looks up at the sea bass mounted on the wall like he's not sure what he's seeing. *It's a sea bass, alright,* I say to him, like we're at the bar. *You can stop guessing.* The coyote stands next to the fireplace, frozen in mid-step. *The heat is warm,* he says. *You should sit by me.* But the heat can't help him, either.

At the house, I lift the lid on the basement freezer. There's a coyote in here, too. The coyote has an arrow buried deep between his eyes. His lips are pulled up in seizure. I call it a "he" but I don't know for sure.

A new one comes in for her first, with her wrists all cut up. She shows us. She smells like she's been at it all day. It wafts off her skin when I hug her, it slicks all over me. Now it is me saying it, parroting: *keep coming back. Keep coming back. Keep coming back.* And the worst—*it gets better.*

I pray for her, *the still sick and suffering,* but I don't see her the next day, or the day after that.

There are guns everywhere at the house. There is a gun as tall as me hung up above the fireplace. An antique piece. I sit my root beer bottle on a pelt that covers the coffee table. The pelt moves with small bugs that crawl around on their little missions. There are guns lined up against a windowsill, fourteen in all. The china cabinet, the one with no glass on the doors—it is full of rifles. Behind a door in the unfinished basement—a rifle. I watch the fire and count the rifles I can see in my peripheral vision. One, two, three.
Four.
Five.

I watch the fire. The logs of wood fall apart as they burn, insides out. Here I am: alive to watch it.

Six.
Seven.

Danger, Will Robinson.

There is someone I could call, but I don't.

When I don't call someone, someone calls me. She asks how I am. *Today didn't kill me.* I say it with a laugh. When I tell her I don't have any fingernails left save the one long pinky nail, she says she's not surprised. She can hear me dragging them down the hillside, she says, even from across the lake. *How much longer do you think you can hold on?* I change the subject. She says I'll learn the kind of honesty that I can live with. Whatever that could feel like, I fear it. When I am *rigorously honest*, like the book says, it feels like sitting too close to the fire when I'm putting wood in, like being readied to blister. I am afraid I'll have to live in this life. She says I should pray. I tell her I'm not above begging for relief. That I'll beg if I need to. *Who said anything about begging? And besides*, she says, *begging isn't honesty.*

•

Ninety days and I want to take my car down to the inlet where the cold creek lets out and watch the water. I want to watch the water slide around like a fissure between worlds. The more you cry, the more you work like water in the world. You lose water and it settles on you. Your skin returns it. Your skin returns you all your poison.

I buy a bottle of root beer. It is the first root beer I drink in years. It is the first bottle I have held Since Then. The last bottle of the last day of the last bottle. I am counting days. I miss holding the glass of the bottle. I lift it like it is nothing and like it is the heaviest part of me. It comes to my mouth or my mouth comes to it.

In the mini-mart I stand in front of The Beer Cave. *Hello, Stella*, I say. I roll the tape. I play it through, slow motion. Reach for her. Use the one long pinky fingernail, the only one unbitten, to jab along the perforated wrapper between the bottle cap bottom and the bottleneck. Peel it away indecorously. Pop off the cap so she can breathe that frosty breath, the one that looks like cartoon smoke from a witch's cauldron.

If I cried alcohol, could I get drunk on myself?

The leaves cake on the water like a rug. Lie down, lie down on the rug like the child you are. Rest your head on your arms and tell yourself a story about a girl in another place, another time, another world. The girl of enchanted forests, the girl whose pain is short-lived because—adventure! An adventure happens.

There is a cake of leaves on the water.

I miss wine most of all. I miss wine and the man who sold me the wine, his wavy gray hair, his British face, the way he scraped off the price tag with a razor blade, the quick *shhhrrkkk* over the smooth glass shoulder. Now that I know I loved you, I miss you even more.

I loved you the length of your rope.

The woozy bobble of the canoe dock mocks me. The water is wet and I am dry.

Bone dry. Desert dry. Without a lick of moisture. Chapped. Weathered as a beaten bone. Deserted lakebed. Pillar of salt. Ancient shore. Fossil. Deep dry. Done in. Dry spell. Fire hazard. Combustible thirst.

·

AT THE HOUSE I WATCH the fire. The embers twinkle and reflect in the coyote's pupils and make his dead eyes shine alive. Not sure what to expect, I touch them. They are all-the-way-hard. What matters is that at a distance, you cannot tell. Lifelike dead thing.

I look at the coyote in the freezer with his arrow. I wonder if anything has been happening to his body. Has it been getting colder, getting all the way frozen? When the arrow hit between the eyes, I imagine there was an instantaneous moment of coagulation. I imagine that when the man gets around to pulling it out, when he peels the coyote skin away from the skull, he will see the blood clumped around the arrow's head. He will see where the animal tried to heal itself. Killing arrows are expensive. When you shoot into the brush, some arrows get lost. *But this one,* the man had said, while tapping an identical one in his hand, *I know right where it landed.*

At the house I open the kitchen freezer. It is filled with turkeys wrapped in butcher paper. I take the stopper off the bottle of the man's bottle of whiskey that sits in the door. I hold it to my nose and breathe it in. I give myself five deep breaths.

When I am rigorously honest and tell her about this, she says *this is your disease tugging at you.*

I keep coming back. She tells me to pray, because *no human power can relieve you.*

The man had been out for Thanksgiving turkeys with his bow. The coyote—an accident of a perfect opportunity, a perfect close range shot. Maybe he will skin it, stuff it, and sell it to the biology lab at a local school. The man prefers the bow hunt, he says it's more humane. *People don't mind wasting bullets. You've only got so many arrows.* It's the lazy hunters that will hobble a deer, break its leg, let it run and starve to death. With arrows there's no point, he says, in shooting an animal in the intestines, to let it wander around the forest for days bleeding to death, unable to eat or drink, your arrow in its gut, snagging on underbrush. *With a bow, you're not going to take a shot that isn't a kill shot.* Guns are traumatic, he says. They are explosive. He makes a "boom" sound with his mouth to emphasize how gunshots scare everything around. *These* (he taps the arrow in his hand), *these are incredibly sharp.* He says it's like when you cut yourself on a just-sharpened knife, but don't notice until you've flung blood across the cutting board, the sink, the refrigerator door. The deer will startle, as if at a bee sting or a long thorn, and continue eating. Then it sinks down, and the others look around but keep moving. The deer can't get up and there won't be time to know why. It is quiet and they are not afraid.

Months later I see her again, the newcomer. She is alive. Her wrists are healed and she appears to me like a mirage, smoking a cigarette and tanned with summer. I put my hand on her arm, as if to test her realness. Husband gone, car wrecked, job lost. I tell her I've prayed for her. Out of rehab, newly blonde, living with her mother but she's never felt better. *Except these*, she says, waving the cigarette and grinning, *I can't quit these!* Stupidly, I tell her it's one thing at a time as she hurriedly stomps it out, not wanting to keep her mother waiting. She gets into the car and I don't see her again.

The man did get his arrow out, but he never skinned the coyote for its pelt. He tossed it down the steep hill where all the year's carcasses went. Winter carries them away, tendon by tendon. I go to toss the compost down the hill and my eye catches the coyote halfway down the slope to the creek, him and the rest of the bone pile, bucks and turkeys, in permanent stagger. Around him, just junk: rusted mattress springs, cinderblocks, empty milk cartons. Now arrowless, the coyote's dulling fur catches in the yellow light. Dead, he is the color of old foam. I imagine his face from here, the dark lips, but I don't step any closer. I pray. Dead for so long now and he still looks frozen, even with the promise of spring.

ERIC PANKEY

To Confirm the Earth's Rotation

Days like drops of mercury merge,
The particular subsumed into the general
And soon there is no unoccupied space.
The past, so it seems, vast, everlasting:
No room for attic, crawl space, or cellar,

Not to mention the junk we've gathered,
Imagining a beach house furnished one day,
Or selling the inherited antiques when
The economy turns around, demand returns.
How far away yesterday retreats, a frontier

Of fogs and icy rain, oddly out of fashion,
Quaint, devoid of nostalgia or ache.
We lived there once and have moved on,
We say. Yet there it is: impinging,
Invasive, like a vine you cut back each summer

But returns the next year more vigorous,
Tangled, determined, weighing down
The azaleas, the dogwood, the camellias,
The cultivated rough edge of the yard
Gone more rough, a realm of weeds

With which the vine will also have its way.
American English could use a word like
Whilst to capture the waylaid hurry that is
Today, now already headlong, relinquishing
The present tense to the past, the *is* to *was*,

The *will be* theorized, but only in books.
We will walk the broken trail up around
The headlands to watch the water's
Green translucence and bright froth unbraid,
And the sun, to confirm the earth's rotation,

Will hesitate and swell before it slips into the deep,
Or maybe it stalls there, hovers as if
To commemorate some rare solar effect—
Flares, dark spots, an aurora's array—
Those who came before knew enough to heed.

CHRISTOPHER SANTIAGO

tu • la

Nahuatl: near the cattails; ruined Toltec capital. Tall atlantes, sun-cut shields. God-nest. Birdsong. Mongolian: willow-banked tributary of the Orkohn. Baltic: unreach-able, Russified to oblast. Ironworks. Hollow points. Music box gilt & nielloed with orchids, islands, passerines; tula-work. Chileno: slang for cock. Also nightshade, bell flower. Solfége: veil & a sixth. English: square-rigged for new continents. Almost marsh grass, ghosted to Caddo. Kotule: savanna tongue, rich in affix, in use by all gen-erations. Sanskrit: Libra. Scales, stars above our son. *Was* the weight of *will*. Nahuatl from the Nahuatl for "what pleases the ear." Tagalog: an aporia. Mother tongue: a poem.

Hele

little monsoon
little fist
& groundswell

they lay you out in naked light
tagged like an ashy thrush

little stroke   little blood-peal
riptide
displaced by a scissor kick

there are no more oceans to cross
just the same we'll let you go

but not today
today

you are a room
words crisp as fresh-cut eyelets

today you are a bell
pitched just high of mine

so that when I sound we sway
like boats

no blood conduction   no diastole

still you recognize the shoreline
unshrouded
beaten bronze

what we sang to you each night

you fold it in your hand
it cools   keeps

even far out of earshot
even deep
in a chirring shoreless continent

ADAM CHILES

My Father's Hearing Aid

seemed lost without his ear, a silenced spigot,
adrift without a doorway, without
the organ's alluvial crib. For years it was you
I spoke to, my calls transfigured, rendered clear
inside your daily minister, amplified.
It was you who fathered me, lifting my words
into the stirrup of his ear, the body's anvil.
You he reached for each morning, sky
unfolding in him then like a canto, birds
hived in the Wisteria, their gossip making sense
once more as though it were something
undeniable, unstoppable out there, transfused,
striking the Sistine of his ear.

My Father's Hearing Aid

has taken its place in my mother's ear, a rectifying machine.
It pleases her with its incoming lecture of wrens.
She smiles, encounters through my father's ear, a morning's debris.
Theatrical, costume-like the way she puts in her ear, another ear.
As though the ear consoles.
As though a wren might put an end to annihilation.
Inch its song into her, sound as grace.
As though my father is listening as her body hums
the motor's inscrutable prayer.

At night the ear is silent, an appliance of stupor.
Tomorrow resumes its audible fury.
Dials her once again into a presence of birds, and the rain's devotional.
The future unfolds its minutes.
And she sits, for a good while, interrogating.
She listens, both ways.
Nothingness grows prodigious, branches down there.
The ear can see. And she whispers
periodically at the patterns of his chair.

HENRY CRAWFORD

The Man Who Understood Television

In his final days ■ my dad ■ got to watch a lot of TV ■
up in the ward ■ a black plastic box ■ bolted to a pipe
mounted to the ceiling ■ emitting ■ aerosol sprays
and prostate pills ■ in steaming bowls ■ of oatmeal ■
(and sometimes soup) ■ earnest little pep rallies ■
for cars and cola ■ white-coated doctors ■ book-faced lawyers
■ sex-crazed detectives ■ freeze-dried spokesmen ■
". . . has this ever happened to you?" ■

He learned ■ the schedules ■ what was coming next ■
■ the consolation prizes ■ the pocket-sized happiness ■
the instantaneous relief ■ and grief ■ of the channel changer
■ he saw how things ■ repeat ■ how they get the smile ■
■ exactly right ■ all teeth ■ white ■ and beautiful ■
on ecstatic women ■ pitching panty hose ■
on a long game show afternoon ■

He came to imagine the producers ■ he could see ■
the executives planning their shows ■ the schedules
■ he saw them calling in their assistants ■ holding hands
they were moving in circles now ■ singing jingles ■
■ rotating in light ■ holding up boxes of fruit flavored flakes ■
going up in balloons ■ scaling ■ the ceilings of Manhattan ■
now it was all sky ■ Central Park erupting in soap suds ■
the heartbeat of America ■ beating time ■
the well-wishers arriving ■ calling for an encore
■ coast to coast ■ a washer ■ a dryer ■ a family sedan ■
my dad once more ■ at the wheel ■ doing his best Gregory Peck ■
his shows brimming over ■ harmonious fields
■ of RGB color ■ in steady streams of electromagnetic waves ■
spreading wide ■ and leaving the Earth in another kind of light ■

SUSAN TICHY

Another Haunting, the Pencil Line

that shimmers under paint, goes on
into the raw paper : the way
imagined but never walked, or never walked
  again : the shape
of ridge and stormcloud, ridge and scree,
the hand alone descending
to paper's edge: the melancholy,
  endless what-ifs
of Ruskin's unfinished drawings:
curve of a snow-chute,
match-stick pine trunks
  fallen or flung:
'the most magnificent piece of ruin
I have yet seen,' or
  beds of limestone bent like a rainbow
  ('a fine accomplice to metaphysics')
  ('erodes according to first flaws')
: pockets of detail, unsurrounded,
like stones from a tricklet—
red pebble the size of two match heads
laid on paper, traced in lead,
  the tracings caught
in same vortex, sprindrift
haunting the highest ridges.
  And where in this body
is pain to be found? Down here,
in too-dense, drought-wrought forest:
the way imagined but never walked,
or never walked again.

OKLA ELLIOTT

The unicyclist has found love at last.

She came to this small Pennsylvania town
on a nearly empty bus
late at night, with stars bursting the sky brightly.
She sang and was perhaps happier
for her singing, perhaps not.
She trained hour upon wobbling hour
and even learned to juggle while riding.
Her balance and poise and dexterity
aroused many amorous thoughts
among the lovers of spectacle.
But lovers of spectacle cannot be loyal.
Then one day, an overcast summer morning in fact,
she was picking the choicest red plums
and placing them carefully
in a wrinkled brown paper bag.
She looked up, neither by design nor by accident,
and saw a man with a beautiful tattoo along his arm
and a confused look on his face. He was fingering gently
a red plum, pondering its future possibilities
as though he had forgotten about the existence of red plums
until that moment.
At first the unicyclist wished she had her unicycle, leotard,
and juggling pins.
Then she was happy that she did not.

JUSTIN BOENING

As You Left It

I suppose it would have been hilarious
had they allowed me to live
forever, paying in divine wisdom
for all my erotic massages,
tipping the jazz quartet
with whatever cocktail coaster
I'd scribbled on the night before,

but it's even stranger here,
now, feeling the cool air
as the concierge kicks me
through the kitchen's
steel back doors, the cruise ship
shoving off from the dock
without me, into the moon-
pocked waves, the stubborn mists,
anything as meaningless
and impossible to imagine as us,

and in the end what drives me nuts
is knowing what I never
thought possible—that when
one returns to his body,
his body will be as he left it,
meaning nakedness on a man
is always a comedy—
and wondering not whether
they'll have me back
but why, and who will be there
waiting to forgive me
for giving up again.

Nobody

When you find me a wreck,
                    curled in weird flowers,
don't wake me; tell nobody I'm here,

that you love me because you love anyone
                    who plans to leave you, that the lies
you've used against me are different

from the lies you've used against yourself,
          that by remaining here, unthinkably still,
we'll be moving closer to the mountains

we've always wanted to be
                              (the ones that weird disguises),
that nobody gifted us this sad

talent, that if our eyes were windows,
                    they were also mirrors reflecting back
nobody's ineffable vanity,

that nobody is who we send when you send
                    our apologies, that nobody has written
the ending we want for ourselves.

TRACI BRIMHALL

Murder Ballad in the Arctic

IN A FJORD, THE HALF-DECOMPOSED remains of a juvenile seal and the skeleton of a pup on its back. On the short cliffs, the bones of a bird I can't identify. I catalog the dead I can name—puffin, narwhal, walrus. Near my foot, a fly, the only living thing. So rarely am I in a place that would kill me, and this one can in so many ways. Everyone here praises the landscape, tosses about *sublime* and *inspired* on the deck of the ship as they polish their camera lenses or write postcards home, but can't they see the rapture could pull our guts from our bellies with its beak, or club us on the head and leave us on a polar beach to rot? The wind is cold and incessant and everything in me wants to live.

•

I THOUGHT THE ARCTIC SUMMER, that region of never-night, might be a place I could write about my friend's murder and the child I'm carrying. I thought the ice caps could teach me what it might mean to wander as punishment for murder or what dreams might look like to my son, who's never seen color and never known fear, but all I see is glacier, mountain, sea, glacier, mountain, sea, glaciermountainsea.

I haven't yet felt my son move, and even though I have a grainy sonogram as proof he is attached and unfurling, he is as abstract to me as God or death. I try to make him real by writing him lullabies, but they all end up being about loss or land-scapes that won't put my child to sleep—cactuses used for target practice, bullet casings jingling like spurs in the tumbleweeds, the canyon roads I used to drive at night and roll the headlights back to see how long I could travel that speed in the dark and remain alive.

•

IN HIS ESSAY ON LULLABIES, Frederica Garcia Lorca said: "Various crucial elements are involved in lulling the child to sleep, including, of course, the consent of the fairies. The fairies bring the windflowers and the right climate. The mother and the song supply the rest." I don't know what an arctic fairy might look like, though I imagine Cain's son with wings and a seal's spinal cord for a wand. Something made of magic and fear bearing purple saxifrage and a mild polar evening. In the lullaby I compose for my son, I write, *Before Socrates drank the hemlock, he washed his body to save his loved ones the trouble.* All my rhymes call to mind Macbeth's witches, which may be as close to Lorca's consenting fairies as I can get. Double the toil. Double the bubble. Triple the ruin. Unknot the couple.

•

SOMEONE PULLS A SEA ANGEL out of the ocean and puts it in a jar on the deck of our ship. It is small and translucent, flapping its wings and turning slow circles in the glass. The angels are hermaphrodites. Lately, polar bears have been born with both sets of sex organs, too, but unlike the angels, hermaphroditic polar bears cannot reproduce. Like most things about this place, it makes me think of an abstinent god, a bored sublimity. Oh, to be everything and unable to create.

I drop a sea butterfly, the angel's mollusk cousin, into the jar, and the angel's gentle flutter turns vicious. Its translucent mouth grows large, rapacious. Always the comfort of a quick and necessary death—to know our life could be snatched away in seconds, but it isn't. Instead, the seal. Instead, the snow bunting. Instead, the jellyfish dead against the rocks, as slick and purple as the ocean depths that gave it up.

•

MY CABIN MATE ON THE ship once investigated how women's murders were consistently reported to take place in beautiful locations. Often times these "beauty spots" weren't that beautiful at all but the newspapers used lyrical descriptions to heighten the romantic horror of the death. Somehow it made the story more scintillating—a picturesque location, a lovely woman, a murderer prowling the park benches with endearments and a piano wire. My cabin mate says the "beauty spot" murders are even more sinister because a woman's body in nature is one of the tropes of pastoral poetry—the woman's body available for wooing and erotic encounter. I wonder if the newspaper reporters covering the discovery of these women's bodies thought of love poems as they drank their coffee, wrote their copy late into the night, and fantasized about their readers.

I think that perhaps I'm guilty of this same need for beauty in death. I've tried imagining my friend's murder in a way that seemed peaceful, a quick release. I've even written about it with the same fetish for beauty. His body in a field, under stars, the sawgrass rustling in the late spring breezes. I wonder if the song I'm writing for my son has Betelguese and Bellatrix, those dual spring stars, burning in it. If it has field and grass and wind. If it has wool and bell in it, or if it has a darker twins—a shadow under the water and three rows of teeth, or an ice field and empty pockets, or a highway in a car squeezed between two strangers who say they don't want to hurt you.

"A dead person is deader in Spain than anywhere else in the world. And whoever wants to leap into dream wounds their feet on the edge of a barber's razor," Lorca said, though he'd never been to the arctic. Still, the icy water leaks through my boots and I lean into the beauty at dream's edge.

•

MINUTES OF SILENCE AND WIND and rain and oblivion so goddamn still and needing nothing. Here, the oblivion is white and cold and has so little to do with joy. I don't know what each person on the ship is learning about themselves, but we are all learning about the north—the names of its flowers, the dangers of its mating birds, the sound of glaciers preparing to calve. The wind won't quit, the rain has joined it, and everyone is quietly photographing the shack of a trapper who lives there all year alone.

•

IN THE NEW LULLABY I write for my son, I want to teach him about the world, not to "plunge the child fully into raw reality, imbuing it with the drama of the world" like Lorca suggested, but to teach him the rhythms of the tradewinds, or how arctic terns travel from the arctic to the Antarctic every year. How well they must know the oceans. How tireless they must be. I want to teach him how to fashion his own splint if he falls while hiking, how to debride a wound. I want to say there are butterflies that drink tears, but instead of the world, I give him what I know of surviving love and the dangers of beautiful places: *Once, an illicit affair was cut short by a romance, but this was before your father, in a desert where the wind whipped my eyes until moths arrived on my cheeks to drink the sweet, sweet salt.*

•

ALL THE BOOKS I READ on the ship are about survival. There are how-to books about knots, advice on sailing, descriptions of how lost explorers traversed the pack ice. Sometimes the bones of sailors are found. Sometimes their whole bodies are preserved in sheets of ice, the dog hair still on their coats, the pictures of beloveds still in their pockets. There's no clear answer about how long a murderer could wander in this landscape if he was exiled here—days, weeks, months, though his chances for survival improves if he is not alone. People used to be condemned to exposure and locked in the stocks. If they lasted a week, there was a chance to be pardoned. I look at the three mugshots and try and imagine who would make it the longest in exile. Who looks like they could bear the cold and rain and hunger and sublime loneliness of a banishment on ice? I decide it is the one whose name I once wanted to give my son.

•

WE COME ACROSS AN ICE floe and anchor the ship. Everyone takes turns walking across the ice and painting, writing or performing. I watch a man in a gorilla suit and space helmet dance without any music. A woman wears a second body on top of her, the broken body her double, her doppelganger, her past. Another woman undresses and poses inside the frame of a cube. She crouches inside the box until her feet bleed and someone brings her clothes. I feel so limited. All I have are lines for lullabies I could never sing to my son. I wish I had three orange cones and a knife. I could lay inside that triangle and ask someone to report the news of my death. Make it beautiful so people will want to hear it, make it sad so they remember, make everyone who hears about it want to deserve the life they've been given.

•

"IN MELODY, AS IN SWEET things, history's emotion finds refuge," Lorca said, "its permanent light free of dates and facts." I want that for my son. I want that for myself. A song free of April, of receipts, of knives in between ribs. I want to unsee where his body was recovered a month after he went missing—browning grasses, weary palms, a storage unit and two cranes in the distance, a gentle hill. The soil under him, rich. Around the star his body made, new shoots thriving.

GEORGE BROOKINGS

The Mountain

OSMA'S WIFE, NADINE, APPROACHED SILENTLY in her sandaled feet and salmon-colored shift with a glass of fresh, iced lemonade in one hand and in the other a shallow, steaming bowl of saltah. It was hot already. The heat had come early this year and the mountains surrounding the city shimmered in the haze of mid-day. As he did most days, Osma dozed in a dusty arm chair under the shade of the blue awning that fronted the brown brick house. The chair was turned to face the great peak of Jabal Sabir.

Why? Nadine had asked him one day, wondering what he saw in the barren promontory. Why do you stare at the mountain. What do you see there? The view, he said, simply. Of course, it was more than that, although he lacked the energy to explain it. If he were to try, he might say something about the majesty implied in such a long existence. Jabal Sabir had risen in that spot even before God created man or beast. He could tell her that. It was one of his first and grandest creations. It did his heart good to know it was there and that he sat at its feet, a pure thing with no sin or evil in it, its eye always filled with the presence of God above. But he did not say any of that. If he had started, Nadine would only have shrugged and accused him of being a dreamer, wasting his time. The mountain was hot and dusty, she would say, and an old man like him could never be comfortable on its rugged slopes. Even if he could get there.

She meant well Osma knew. She loved him and wanted to spare him pain.

A fan buzzed beside him, pulsing the 90 degree air and creating a current of cooler air. He heard the door slam shut as Nadine came out of the house. She had been cooking and placed a warm bowl in his lap and a dish on the table beside him. She meant to tempt his elusive appetite with the spicy aromas of meat stew, scrambled eggs and freshly baked flat bread, hot from the oven. She had learned not to ask him if he was hungry.

That was one benefit of dying; he was never hungry. Food was unnecessary to the culmination of that process, already well advanced in his case. And on those rare occasions when he was tempted to eat as he once did, his body reminded him that he needed little or no sustenance by expelling the excess from his stomach.

Osma's body ached with fatigue. His clothes hung on him and a nagging, persistent cough came and went on its own mysterious schedule from some place deep in his lungs. He had not yet divulged to Nadine that his gums were sore and bleeding. Soon, the doctor had said on his last visit to Sana'a, his teeth would go, if his kidneys didn't fail first. But he did not feel sorry for himself at all. It was Nadine who filled his mind with worry about the future. She was the reason he sat facing the placid mountain, trying to learn from it. Of course he could not say any of this. He did not wish to alarm her. But neither would it be right to indulge her in the comfortable pretence that he would recover, as many of those who came to visit were apt to do.

You are looking better, such people would say, lying with the best of intent, to cheer him up. It was they who needed comfort, however spurious, in the presence of death. He did not blame them. After all, he had brought it on himself. No, he did not regret that he might have lived another twenty years. He had already experienced all that was fit for a man to know. More important to Osma now was the knowledge that his death would count for something. That was more than most men could say. "It is for the Ummah that you aided us. For God, remember that," Dr. Ansari had confided to him, after the work and the damage had been done. "Your name will live forever."

Almost one year had passed since the mysterious Dr. Ansari first appeared at his door, in the company of Osma's brother-in-law, Nijad. Dr. Ansari was a Saudi, tall, thin, with graying hair and thick eyeglasses. He was a little stooped over, perhaps an old back injury that still plagued him, as all men were subject to accumulating wear and misfortune. The two men refused the offered black tea or coffee with many apologies and Nadine took it back. It was not the custom here to reject hospitality, nor to conduct business without first meeting each other as men. We are en route to another destination and already late, Dr. Ansari explained, aware of the breach of custom. Could he see the workshop? He had a project that he wished to discuss.

Osma had been at some pains to conceal his surprise. In retrospect it was the first of many signs that this was not like other business he had secured in Ta'izz. But he was eager for work and proud to show the two men the half-cylinder aluminum structure that housed an array of precision German metalworking equipment ranged around its perimeter. As the men followed Osma, he explained the functions and capabilities of the ovens, casting and bending machines, drill presses, metal lathes and precision grinding equipment. Along the walls he showed them his work benches, full of neatly stored hand tools. Bins and overhead storage held raw lengths of steel and aluminum awaiting the reshaping that gave them purpose.

Dr. Ansari listened carefully and respectfully. He looked at everything, his eyes wide open as if to absorb and remember. He asked what kinds of work Osma did here. About Ta'izz and the customers who came here to have metal fabrication work done for them. It is not Sana'a or Aden, he told them, but a large city nonetheless and there was enough work to support such a shop.

"Do you do such work for the authorities of Yemen?" The question was delivered gently, but, still, it was unexpected, odd. When Osma hesitated, the doctor resumed quickly, without waiting for an answer. "I am too curious, I know," he apologized, smiling. "It is not important." He did not say so, but Osma concluded after many such questions and answers that Dr. Ansari was not an engineer, and certainly not a metallurgist.

They came full circle to a cluttered desk full of books, manuals, catalogues and other materials that stood near the entrance. Adjacent to the desk was a flat, aluminum drawing table under a bank of overhead lights.

"May I?" Dr. Ansari asked Osma, reaching into a large briefcase and unfolding a set of drawings, then laying them flat on the table. He held out an open palm in invitation. He wished Osma to look at the drawings.

Osma pressed a rocker switch and four lamps cast a soft, consistent light on the table and the drawings, illuminating the first schematic: a simple disc, or cross section of a cylinder. A smaller disk was to be cored from the center, yielding a ring of metal.

"There will be five more like this," the Doctor said. Osma had already noted the quantity in the detailed specifications inscribed at the bottom of the page. He nodded and turned the page to the second drawing. This one depicted a rod—a "spike," the doctor termed it -- that would exactly fill the hollowed centers of the six rings.

"The engineers tell me that there can be no gaps or cavities." He looked at Osma expectantly.

"Yes, I see that, Doctor. The work will call for precision."

Despite his answer, Osma remembered thinking how surprisingly simple the thing was. The sequence of steps was as clear to Osma then as the barren promontory of Jabal Sabir was now. But this simplicity was in its own way a puzzle. And one that he could not address directly. He remembered wanting to ask why they did not use one of the many capable metal fabricators who served the giant oil companies in the eastern part of the Kingdom, far closer to Riyadh. Perhaps the doctor expected to pay much less for the work here in Yemen. Of course, he knew the reason now. But on that day he had been very eager to have the contract, too eager to let his thoughts stray or to ask awkward questions.

He had instead returned to the packet of drawings and methodically examined the rest in silence while his two guests waited. These drawings too called for fabrication of relatively simple shapes: two hollow cubes of different sizes and a variety of smaller parts that appeared to be brackets or supports, some of which he might be able to buy rather than make himself.

"It seems simple enough," Osma declared at last.

"It is the fine tolerances that require your advanced skills," Dr. Ansari amended pleasantly. "As well as complete discretion. I am sorry to emphasize that and I mean no disrespect."

The good doctor was a reader of faces, Osma realized with chagrin.

"I understand," Osma answered, careful not to freight his words or expressions with question marks or idle curiosity. "But the project is well within my capabilities." He did not have to say that he would be discrete.

"Excellent. The work is yours, if you want it."

"I thank you," Osma answered, smiling and relieved.

"We will be in contact when the materials are ready. As for payment, Nijad will agree to pay whatever you think is fair. You will name your price."

That, he had not expected. Being told to name his price. Such a strange way to do business. But he had the work. They had shaken hands. That was the main thing.

After the visit of Nijad and Dr. Ansari, two whole months passed without a word from either man. Osma resigned himself to the fact that something had changed. Plans were modified and budgets shrank. He had seen it happen before; the expansive dreams of men exceeding their financial reach. Or a project might fall to a competitor with better connections. But then the phone rang one day after dinner. Nadine answered, smiling broadly. It was Nijad. "I am coming," he told them, "about the work we discussed."

The next day a dusty red Toyota pickup truck pulled into the yard. It was Nijad and he was in the company of two burly, unsmiling young men, Saeed and Samir—his assistants, he called them. Osma watched as the three of them unloaded a modest, but surprisingly heavy, wooden crate and wrestled it into the shop on a dolly. They closed and locked the shop doors. Then pried off the crate's wooden cover, sprung nails clinking haphazardly to the concrete floor. Despite the gloom of the poorly lighted entry space, Osma saw why the crate had been so heavy. Layers of lead sheathing lined the interior. And at the bottom, bubble wrapped, as if they had been delicate, fossilized dinosaur eggs, lay ingots of a gray metal. Osma picked one up. It too was surprisingly heavy and oxidized under the packing materials with a white and pale yellow rime. Even though he had not worked this metal before, he knew what it was. He was surprised and a little frightened. But he made sure that his face showed nothing. If they had wished to invite questions on this topic, they would have done so before this. There was nothing useful to be said.

He set to work the same day. After the long delay, only a single week had been allotted to complete the task and fashion the components. While he did not understand the sudden urgency, he knew questions would not be welcomed or answered. Besides, he was sure it could be done in one week if he worked diligently. He drew up the work plan and reviewed it. It was still simple and his approach was sound. He would first carefully clean the ingots of the oxidation, then fire and cast the basic shapes. Finally, he would cut, core, file and polish the major parts until they matched the exacting dimensions specified in the drawings. The subsidiary parts would need some bending, but there the raw material was plain sheet aluminum. A journeyman's task.

As he worked, one of the twins—as his neighbors had taken to calling Nijad's bearded assistants, even though they looked not at all alike—was always in the shop, watching his progress. They did not engage him in conversation, but spoke softly to each other. The twin not in the shop would smoke outside or take a seat at a nearby cafe. They were polite, but not friendly. I cannot tell you, they would answer a curious neighbor when asked almost any question about themselves or the work Osma was doing for them. Beneath the politely delivered refusals those who asked also heard a muted warning that their questions were not welcome. The neighbors complained. Nadine called Nijad to object to such rudeness. No insult is intended, he assured her; please apologize to your friends and neighbors, but the work is secret. They act only as they have been instructed to act. You must forgive them. "We must protect the project from our competition," Nijad explained. "They would steal it if they could."

Despite the tight schedule, the work went smoothly, with only one minor difficulty. It was the mask and clumsy breathing apparatus Nijad had brought for Osma. For the dust, Nijad had explained. The equipment impeded Osma's movements and the mask fogged over in the humidity of the shop. He could not see his tools or instruments clearly and thus risked making a foolish error and ruining the work. He had removed the elaborate breathing equipment and donned a simple cloth medical mask and goggles instead. Only later was the cost of that decision apparent.

When his cough began producing blood, long after the work had been delivered, he finally consented to be driven to the hospital in Sana'a by a neighbor. The doctor showed him the chest X-ray, pointing to the regular shapes of white rib bones obscured by irregular zones of opacity, as if tiny clouds had become trapped in his chest cavity. The occlusions did not look dangerous to Osma, but the radiologist's face reminded him of a day long ago, when his father had kneeled down, eye to eye with eight-year old Osma, and informed him that his mother had died giving birth to his sister. His father and sister had passed on, years ago. Now it was his turn.

When Osma broke the news to his wife that his illness was not a stubborn virus or some new allergy, she had cried.

"It is God's will," Osma said to comfort her. But she continued to cry, even though it was God's will.

Nijad scolded him too, sounding almost angry. "Why did you not use the apparatus?" he complained. And then, "You should have called me first. I could have taken you to a better hospital, in the Kingdom. I will speak to the doctors in Sana'a."

Still, after all, Osma had done something momentous. Something that would change the world. That was what Dr. Ansari had said when he called. Osma should take solace in those words. No man would remember him for the awnings he made or the fanciful gilded cages he built for a rich collector of tropical birds, the doctor added, showing a much more detailed knowledge of Osma's business than he had suspected. This work was larger than one man's life.

But when Osma repeated these words to Nadine, her dampened spirits were not lifted and the tears flowed again. He resolved not to speak of it again. It was a hard thing for a husband or a wife to be left behind and selfish to expect complicity.

Nadine held out a glass of sugary lemonade with its dripping condensation. She could be stubborn, even fierce, in defense of him. There was no point in refusing. He took the glass—heavier than he expected—and sipped a few drops of the bitter-sweet liquid while she waited. Unlike many of his neighbors who had empty, soulless marriages bound by duty, he loved his wife and was all the more sorry for the pain he caused her. He trusted that Nijad would ensure that the shop and its contents sold for a fair price and that Nadine would have what she needed. Of course, in the end, it was all in the hands of God. Nothing happened that was not His will. Who was Osma to argue against this most fundamental truth of human existence?

And the mountain agreed with him. Not that it said so in words, but in its posture; never changing its complexion or hiding behind clouds. A mountain was better than a man in this respect. It lacked the capacity for embarrassment or regret, being whole and perfect. That was what he would tell Nadine if she ever asked him again about the mountain and why he looked at it.

Then it came to him. He would go to the mountain. Not today, but soon. He would say to her, this mountain is what a man would be if he were wise enough. Perhaps it would speak to him in its own voice if he went there and listened carefully. He felt that close to it. It had been there his whole life, watching him, longer than his mother and father. But even as the thought came to him, inspired him, he knew he could not say anything of the sort to Nadine. That was a problem; it had always been so. There were things she would not want to hear. She would plant her feet, put her hands on her hips. She would be thinking of smaller things. That he should die so young. That he would leave her, with little enough to get by on. She would never think to ask him about the silvery white metal he had shaped. Or wonder if it had come from the earth of Jabal Sabir itself. Or what the mountain might think of that. The mountain that did not change and had always been the same.

The finely honed rings and spikes, now assembled into something with a purpose, must already be on the way, he thought. Of course they would not tell him what or where or when, but everyone would know when it arrived. When that day came, and the silvery metal did what it was meant to do, he wondered if the mountain would approve or if it would maintain its stony silence and indifference to the doings of men. There was a chance that afterwards it would not welcome him as a brother. That it would say, you profess to admire my stillness and perfection, and yet you have introduced as great a change into the world as there has ever been, and all the changes that will follow this will also be yours to bear. We must remain ever distant henceforth. Man and mountain.

That was why he sat here. That was what he would tell his wife, if he dared. Perhaps he would leave her a note, so that she would not interrupt him before he was finished. Bringing him more soup, a bit of gossip from the market.

Osma meant to set down the heavy, sweating glass filled with lemonade, but his hand was numb. The glass slipped and fell, the cool yellow liquid sinking into the dust. He watched it soak into the dirt of his small yard in the foothills of Jabal Sabir.

Translation Folio

JERZY FICOWSKI

Translator's Introduction

Jennifer Grotz

OVER THE COURSE OF HIS singular life and career, Jerzy Ficowski (1924-2006) published more than a dozen individual volumes of poetry in Polish, the best known of which is *A Reading of Ashes* (beautifully illustrated by Marc Chagall). In intellectual circles, he is best known as the crucial and primary authority on the expressionist Jewish fiction writer and visual artist Bruno Schulz, who was killed by the Gestapo in 1942. Ficowski studied Schulz's life, drawings, and writing for more than a decade, publishing the first definitive literary biography on Schulz, entitled *Regions of the Great Heresy*. Additionally Ficowski, who took part as a young man in the Warsaw Uprising, travelled with the Polish Roma population after the war and became an avid historian of the Polish Romani as well, documenting their culture in several monographs and also translating their poetry into Polish, especially the work of a woman known as Papusza. For much of his life, he made his living as a popular songwriter, all the while writing and publishing his own poems.

Ficowski's poetry deftly takes on the most sobering of subject matter. Many of his poems confront head-on the events and suffering he witnessed first-hand during World War II and in its long, complicated aftermath in Poland. His work includes purely lyric poems, too, love poems and gorgeous descriptions and meditations on nature and landscape, but his poetry is especially attentive to remembering people lost in the Holocaust. His poems give valuable context and believable emotional testament to twentieth-century Polish life but also to much of human joy and suffering in general, and unlike Tadeusz Różewicz, for example, one of his contemporaries, Ficowski's poetry never fully embraces despair.

That said, and as the translations included here illustrate, Ficowski's poetry is as fascinatingly playful as it is deeply serious. A little like another contemporary, Zbigniew Herbert, Ficowski's poetry is simultaneously austere and linguistically playful and complex. He does unusual and inventive things with language—making nouns into verbs and vice versa, for example—and he also pares language down to its minimum, often eschewing unnecessary words, punctuation, even capitalization. As a poet undertaking these translations, I have felt simultaneously humbled and thrillingly challenged by his work. Ficowski provides access to a definition and embodiment of poetry that just doesn't quite exist yet in English (isn't this always the case in the translation of poetry?). And in the best of his work, there is as extraordinary a marrying of form and content as I have ever encountered in any language.

Working on Ficowski's poetry has been, if amazingly rewarding, a markedly different experience than any of my previous translating, not only because of the rich and idiosyncratic nature of his work but also because all of it has been undertaken with a co-translator, Piotr Sommer. Himself an accomplished poet and exceptional translator of American and British poetry into Polish, Sommer was also a protégé of Ficowski and has been a careful and subtle reader and editor of his poems over decades. Working on these translations with him has necessarily involved numerous and extended conversations about the poems themselves as well as about both the English and Polish languages and the nature of successful literary translation. It has reminded me time and again that although undertaking translation is an act of literary service, it is also a precious act of literary education. I would describe our translation process as decidedly two-fold, stemming from the complexity of Ficowski's poetry and also my own (sometimes differing) poetic sensibility as an American poet as well as my challenges as a non-native reader of his work. The first "movement" of each translation has been making several drafts that render the content and materiality of the poem sufficiently, clearly and coherently. This begins with something like a literal translation that is slowly "tamed" into a very clear and expressive English. The second step or "movement," which itself also takes several subsequent drafts of each poem as well as frequently posing questions to other poets and native speakers of Polish, is a complicating and "unleashing" or untaming of the previous version, as the complexity of the original poem slowly reveals itself and as we begin to see the ways in which the translation can convey as much of the complexity of Ficowski's original as possible while also making a convincing poem in English. The result, poem by poem, has been thrilling.

JERZY FICOWSKI : Five Poems

Penetration

I am not ashamed of tears
I am the undresser of an onion
from her onionish scales
from the gold
violet
green
down to the deep leukoma
in search of
onion
onio
on
And here it turns out
that there is no onion at all
and to such a degree
that the inside
of the multilayered surface
lacks even a place
for emptiness

The Bird Beyond the Bird

Look
the bird is flapping
to escape from itself
it's flinging itself out of the nest of being
it wants to take a break from feathers
to slip out of being a bird

But it's unable
to outpace itself
by even a beak's length

Look
the bird defeated
with its inseparable self
it lands on a branch

The bird on a branch
sings in every direction
reaches seven echoes simultaneously
covers contradictory distances

Look
the bird victorious
throughout the forest

the bird beyond the bird

Thursday

In the very middle of the week there grows a Thursday the color of dust. This is the place of our painlessly creaking stairs, the smoothness of handrails worn slippery by generations of hands. This is the mouse that died under the cupboard awhile back and nothing came of it. All the Thursday butterflies fade to nothing, the mirrors on Thursday repeat us, stammering until extinguished by a white yawn.

At the bottom of Thursday's lows, girls walk listlessly in crooked stockings. And the ghosts of cabbage soups linger in closed stairways.

Thursday creeps under the yellow banners of flypaper, the choral dirges of flies.

Those who forgot about Wednesday and have lost hope in Friday howl at the Thursday moon and pass on. For them, Thursday is eternal.

Entomology

Yellow buzzes, and sharpened
on the light is honey's sting.
Gray whispers—a fur of fire.
In the music of late spheres
the hymenoptera hours revolve
around a lamp oil eternity.
It smokes azurely,
more and more lightly
circles such a blizzard,
such a maze, a mazurka,
as if the prince of the beetles
were playing his own mustache.
A shameless flight, a spinning whirligig
that exposes colors:
shade after shade, astride a breeze.
And in the hexagons
of beeswax:
the Eye of Instinct.
It knows everything.
There's nothing it doesn't know.

Creator

In the morning he created vast fogs
the size of his boredom

Above the waters he placed a night
the color of dirt under a fingernail

Therefore come visit his world
wide as a yawn
Enter through the triumphant door
Ring three times
the great bell

for this night condemned to eternity
for the fog that rots time
for the water struck speechless

Because the green kingdom of frogs
is not of his world

Frogs have their own

And so he has to croak
all on his own
in the nonexistent rushes

Translated from the Polish by Jennifer Grotz & Piotr Sommer

ALEXIS ORGERA

Rocket Android Systems

The dachshund in the video wants nothing
more from the clown. We should all be so lucky.
Night wants fifty-seven inversions of itself,
mostly pocket-sized, most by way of skin.
In the morning, gray light diffuse through windows
taller than me. Dog curled into a C. A man
in his watery bed, looking up. He describes
his research on dopamine & the Parkinson's brain,
& I think of that brain's magnificent
supernova. I've thought about this before, forever,
in every synapse. I've asked & asked myself-slash-
the universe. I know there are only
unsolved equations. To lie for a living,
what would that be like, going to work
every morning to tell all sorts of untruths?
You'd get good at it. You'd want to come home
at night & lie to your children. You'd want to tell them
with certainty that God exists, that he's a man,
that his son was born via earthly vessel
to save us. You'd want to lie to your children
this way, to pray before dinner & teach them
to imagine that glorious moment when they're
dead, holding hands in heaven with reunited kin,
looking down at the liars they left behind.

CHLOE HONUM

The Ward Above

I don't need to look up to know that inside some of the fluorescent lights there are dead flies on their backs, their wings at crisp diagonals. The psychiatrist has a face like an old dictionary. I imagine myself in the ward above, for the more severe cases. I'm afraid I'll float up and ask to be admitted. In the common room, the Vietnam vet says, No, you don't want to go up there. Everything he says, he says again with his eyes. At home, my dog sleeps beside me. She groans as I slide my hand beneath her head. I speak to her. I carry her warm, happy skull through the night.

TIM CARTER

Safety Guidelines for the Snake Department:

Do not make direct eye contact with the snake. Stay at least five feet from the bars of the cage. Approach, if you must approach at all, cautiously, as one does a difficult question. That snakes consist mostly of a single, continuous stomach is a myth; intestines actually make up most of the snake's innards, which is why snakes are so good at things like digesting large game and literary hermeneutics. Some snakes use quick, rhythmic flicks of their tongue to hypnotize potential prey, nestling such words as "ankle" and "ache" between their tiny fangs. For this reason, never apply pressure to what he says. Never walk with him to the end of the cage, or consider the subtext of a trail. Snakes use their elaborately colored scales to further their art. He'll wonder out loud why the builder of the cage thought to use iron bars instead of Plexiglas. Do not think about that question. He'll slither out from the previous sentence as from a discarded skin. He'll ask you if the allegorical nature of this poem is perhaps a bit heavy-handed. If it doesn't all seem a bit too intentional. Perhaps, he'll whisper, drawing you close, you're doing exactly what the poem wants by keeping all your attention on me. Never mind these arbitrary rules casually euphemized as 'guidelines'. Never mind what the poem insinuates about being your own person. Or about how all this works against your assumptions about how a poem should sound. Do not climb into the snake's mouth. Whatever you do, do not. For it is dimly lit, and extends far back in time.

The Pope Jumps the Grand Canyon

"Love," he says, stepping over the seat of his white Harley XR-750 with gold handle-bar tassels, "is often confused with fear. Why am I attempting such a dangerous feat so late in my career? Well, what I like to say is, His mouth is always open." He revs his engine and smiles. "You know, as a young boy I would terrorize my mother. I'd drink my father's liquor, climb trees, and throw myself from the highest boughs. I'd tell her I heard voices when I was up there. Drove her nuts. She used to say, you're a lunatic and someday you'll seriously hurt somebody. You know what I told her? I told her, we fear death because we perceive it as absence, but forget we are only conscious extensions of that absence." Across the canyon, trees shimmer in the heat. "Truth is, I'm more afraid of living than I am of dying." He grows quiet, and adjusts his goggles. "The sky's the perfect thing, you know, for exits. No testimonies left behind, no evidence of your momentary acrobatics. It's full of wounds that always heal."

Current Theories of Infinity

An infinite number of monkeys pressing randomly designated letters of a single type-writer will, in theory, generate a semantically correct sentence faster than would a single monkey randomly pressing keys over an infinite amount of time. Both theories have their problems, but we are very patient. The single monkey, if used, must be constrained in front of the typewriter by a series of belts, or he will out of rage refuse to complete the experiment. Occasionally we must appease the monkey with fabricated news of his family: a curl of hair, a broken stick. Some scientists argue these prompts affect the purity of the writing process, but we are willing to risk everything. The use of an infinite set of monkeys presents an entirely different, mostly practical, problem. Each monkey is to be placed in a bare cell outfitted with a single button. Curiosity as to why the button whispers its existence will ensure it is continuously pressed, or oppressed. The only difficulties are finding an infinite number of monkeys and the construction of the cells themselves, which is arduous and involves extensive underground excavation. Once completed, they resemble hygienic tombs, row upon row of receding skulls, systematically arranged in parallel floors, lit from within.

LANDON GODFREY

Mirror

A deep hole in the wall. An empty well. An excavation. Terrible memory. Every face a surprise. Every time. The ornate frame, half of a long marriage, tells the mirror the same stories over and over, the mirror eager to hear them, but to its depthless mind, repeated stories always sound new. Beautiful but old, could have been silvered just yesterday for all it can remember. So it says. Hidden in the lustrous shine of endless light, the mirror keeps a secret: no lover is completely unlike another.

Museum

Randall Hufbauer, 1965-1990

your paintings ghost-glazed and suspended in the museum of memoryfactured beauty paintings shy like new deer among bare trees nub-antlered yet crowned by visions
of chandeliers swaying dark above their heads why didn't you wait for those candles
to light my cold eyes want to put on your black coat your black coat hanging in the
forest's closet my eyes like beggars in the winter with gloveless hands full of snow and
you saying *eat the snow*

hazuzeM

A woman hangs a cage in a doorway. No bird. The woman sings. In the distance something in the sky. Bird? Thunder? In the cage a parchment that is not a bird whispers. No sky. In the distance something in the distance. Many no birds and many no clouds? In the cage a thunder. In the woman a doorway.

MOLLY SPENCER

Portrait of Hometown as Constellation

That night I learned to see love in a trigger finger—
Dixie coming to finish the job, Dick's horse having slipped
the pasture, having met with a luckworn Ford.
Love in the blessed moan of the six o'clock whistle
calling the men from the fields for supper. Love even
in the way the Baptist preacher stepped across his doorway
to keep me from his house. Love in his voice, 2 Corinthians,
Be ye not yoked with unbelievers. I wanted to say, I do believe.
In the waving quilt of fields shook out and settled here
on earth. And every so often a limping barn,
a slumped house. And every so often a tidy one. I believe
in the way the right-angled roads always ended
at the speck of town on the map—its righteous blocks
and steeples, its tired lake fringed with reeds, the dump
of sand we called the beach. In the water tower, wooden
and dark against a lingering pastel dusk. All summer
with Jane on her parents' porch. Diet cherry 7-UP
and who kissed who for how long where—against
Emmons' barn, out Derby Road, maybe in the meadow
called Tall Tall Grass. I believe in the night
Tracey died, the night Kelley died, the shoe tossed
from a car on the front page and my mother turning
the paper face down on the table. In the songs we sang
after, How great Thou. I believe in all those winter miles
of gym floor Wesley swept at half-time. In the quick flip
of the Bic he pulled from his pocket to light the altar
candles on his wedding day. I believe in my brother
bent and weeping in Jane's hair the day Ty
swallowed his death with a sip of water. I believe
in wood smoke, wind-break, a gravel road strolling along
to a place where the next field is the memory of a field
of stars in the dwindling light. We've tried
to make them ours, pressed our stories on the night's

specked canvas. The northing bear, the hunter, the woman
who talked too much of her own allure. Shape
of all questions—who, what, when (where did Lisa hide
her baby all that time?). Odd-angled beauty, night-strung,
always somewhat upside down. We never knew her name,
would not have known how to say it. I believe
in the way she leans and circles the pole forever, in her
hunched shoulders, stained hand. Erratic, variable. "Given
to occasional outbursts in brightness."

Note: The text in quotes is from the description of the constellation Cassiopeia in *Star Tales*
by Ian Ridpath. New York, NY: Universe Press, 1988.

ANDREW DELOSS EATON

Meditation at Lagunitas Brewery

All the new drinking is about hops.
In this it resembles the old drinking.
The idea that if an object, a barrel of ale,
for example, which carried overseas
is prone to stale, can be obscured
by a mask of floral scents, for instance,
it has been altogether changed. The font
across my coaster peels away, imitating
either a wanted poster or the burnt out hair
and skin from a cattle brand—in biodegradable
paper and ink, it says on the back—is neither,
but rather a moody signifier of them both.
Or the notion that, since industry
is increasingly digital, forms of physicality
including labor even have become nostalgic
in as much as they are willed. By some.
We talked about it last month on FaceTime
and in the voice of my friend there was a thin wire
of spliced static, a tone almost mechanical
in the little speaker on my laptop.
After a while I understood my bandwidth
needed to be wider. There was a road
I watched while my father drove
the brown pickup. Opening the small
triangle-shaped window, I would smell
the tangle of gravel and saltwater, feel
surrounded with presence, like darkness
around a lit match. I wanted to increase,
I wanted to decrease, I wanted to become
him, I wanted never to become him.
Become, I say, since I am full of movement.
Particles of me are even moving now,
the article in the science magazine tells me

before I return it to the stack of them
sitting on the counter. Those street lamps
at the peninsula, a boardwalk the imagination follows
until the daydream turns its open sign to CLOSED.
I hear Citra and Cascade hops release vowels
without language in my throat. The server
draws the shade open on a pit bull
who lifts its head. Outside, a black star
of smartphones on the metal table
pulsing: *listen, listen, listen.*

CHRISTOPHER HOWELL

Religious Experience

Once during a lightning storm at sea
a man danced on the flight deck
and loosed a sort of singing
in a language no one knew.
The MAA's men stood around, confused
and blustering, "Look at that dumb fuck!"
to hide their fear. The lightning
brought his image in jagged,
cinematic flashes
so that at times he appeared to walk
the black air like a demon, like bad news
that was almost there.

And we were, ourselves, such news, an ark
of grey menace, choppers and fighters lined up
two by two and a red glow from the depths
in which we lived, "trampling out the vintage."

The man, Boatswain's Mate Second Class Pendarvis,
danced and danced
until the Captain said, "That's it, get the son-of-a bitch
down to sick bay," and they hauled him off, legs flailing, voice
a leaping genuflection, lightning blasts separating
one moment from the next
as we were, in fact, separate each from what we thought
the world should be.

But Pendarvis danced on, even in sick bay, singing
in Sumerian or Mu, and the Chaplain,
having been sent for, arrived
frowning and helpless as a man of peace on a warship,
which is what he was.

MARK IRWIN

Emaciated white horse, still alive, dragged with a winch cable to be slaughtered.

You must continue to holler this into the YouTube video. —And what
that one eye flickering still registers from sky
between the barn and your screen. *Stop*, I screamed, the long

parameters of that word. *Stop*, I said, till the horse
becomes a house for us all. We live inside the hide
of that archival tent the wind still bellows

wild. *Abracadabra*, I said, to make the whole thing vanish. Sometimes
you need to forget the words

before you can know the feeling. —To push the shovel's tang
polished from each shove
                                into blue soil. To bury

the horse in earth while the galloping white space between words never stops.

Bios

JENNIFER ATKINSON is the author of five poetry collections, most recently *The Thinking Eye* (Free Verse Editions, 2016) and *Canticle of the Night Path* (2012). The recipient of two Pushcart Prizes, she teaches at George Mason University.

ANNE BARNGROVER is the author of *Yell Hand Blues* (Shipwreckt Books, 2013) and co-author, with Avni Vyas, of the chapbook *Candy in Our Brains* (CutBank, 2014). Her work has appeared in *Crazyhorse*, *Ecotone*, *Mid-American Review*, *Third Coast*, and elsewhere. she serves as Contest Editor for *The Missouri Review*.

ANURADHA BHOWMIK is a Bangladeshi-American writer, an MFA candidate at Virginia Tech, and poetry editor for *The Minnesota Review*. She has received a Grin City Collective Emerging Artist Residency, and her work appears in *The Boiler*, *Lunch Ticket*, *Origins*, *Star 82 Review*, and elsewhere.

ADRIAN BLEVINS' poetry collections are *Live from the Homesick Jamboree* (Wesleyan UP, 2009) and *The Brass Girl Brouhaha* (Ausable Press, 2003), which won the Kate Tufts Discovery Award. She teaches at Colby College.

JUSTIN BOENING's poetry collection *Not on the Last Day, But on the Very Last* (Milkweed Editions, 2016) won the National Poetry Series and is forthcoming. His chapbook *Self-Portrait as Missing Person* won a Poetry Society of America National Chapbook Fellowship.

TRACI BRIMHALL is the author of three poetry collections, including the forthcoming *Saudade* (Copper Canyon) and *Our Lady of the Ruins* (W. W. Norton, 2012), which won the Barnard Women Poets Prize. The recipient of an NEA Fellowship, she teaches at Kansas State University.

GEORGE BROOKINGS is working on a collection of short stories and his third novel. He writes from both Fort Lauderdale, Florida, and Lima, Peru.

URSULA BROOKS has declined to provide biographical information.

Poet and critic **STEPHEN** (sometimes also Stephanie) **BURT** is Professor of English at Harvard and the author of several books of poetry and literary criticism, among them *Belmont* (Graywolf Press, 2013); *The Art of the Sonnet*, with David Mikics

(Harvard UP, 2010); and the new chapbook *All-Season Stephanie* (Rain Taxi, 2015). A new book, *The Poem is You: 50 Contemporary American Poems and How to Read Them*, is forthcoming from Harvard University Press in late 2016.

TIM CARTER is pursuing his MFA in poetry at Syracuse University. His poems can be found in *The Alembic*, *This Land Press*, and *Willard & Maple*.

JOHN CHÁVEZ's full-length collection of poetry *City of Slow Dissolve* (University of New Mexico Press, 2012) won the IPPY Award Gold Medal for Poetry. His poems appear in *Diode*, *The Laurel Review*, *Notre Dame Review*, *Puerto del Sol*, and elsewhere.

ADAM CHILES' poetry collection is *Evening Land* (Cinnamon Press, 2008; UK). His poems appear in *Barrow Street*, *Best New Poets*, *Gulf Coast*, *Indiana Review*, and elsewhere. He teaches at Northern Virginia Community College.

CHARLIE CLARK's poetry has appeared in *Best New Poets*, *The Missouri Review*, *Pleiades*, *Threepenny Review*, and elsewhere. He lives in Austin, Texas.

HANNAH CRAIG is the author of the poetry collection *This History That Just Happened* (Free Verse Editions, 2016), which won the New Measure Poetry Prize. Her poems appear in *North American Review*, *Prairie Schooner*, *Southampton Review*, and elsewhere.

HENRY CRAWFORD works as a software engineer. His poetry has appeared in *BlazeVox13*, *Borerline Press*, and *InSteroPress*.

ANDREW DELOSS EATON was born in California and lives in Belfast, Northern Ireland. His poems appear in *Hayden's Ferry Review*, *Narrative*, *Poetry Ireland Review*, and elsewhere. In 2016 he won the Tupelo Quarterly Poetry Prize, selected by Tracy K. Smith.

OKLA ELLIOTT's books include the poetry collection *The Cartographer's Ink* (NYQ Books, 2014), the short story collection *From the Crooked Timber* (Press 53, 2011), a translation of Jürgen Becker titled *Blackbirds in September* (Black Lawrence Press, 2015), and *Bernie Sanders: The Essential Guide* (Eyewear Publishing, 2016). He teaches at Misericordia University.

Poet, songwriter, and critic **JERZY FICOWSKI** is best known for his critical and biographical monograph on the fiction writer Bruno Schulz. For more information on Ficowski, see page 133.

STEPHEN GIBSON is the author of six collections of poetry, the most recent of which are *The Garden of Earlthly Delights Book of Ghazals* (Texas Review Press, 2016) and *Rorschach Art Too* (Story Line Press, 2014), which won the Donald Justice Prize.

LANDON GODFREY is the author of *Second-Skin Rhinestone-Spangled Nude Soufflé Chiffon Gown* (Cider Press, 2011), which David St. John selected for the Cider Press Review Book Award. Her poems appear in *Beloit Poetry Journal*, *Best New Poets*, *Bombay Gin*, *The Collagist*, and elsewhere. She co-edits, -designs, and-publishes *Croquet*, a postcard letterpress broadside hand-printed on a vintage Kelsey, and lives in Black Mountain, NC, with her husband, poet Gary Hawkins.

Former manager of the Sarajevo Film Festival, **PAULA GORDON** translates from Bosnian, Croatian, Montenegrin, and Serbian. She lives in Wilmington, Delaware.

Poet and translator **JENNIFER GROTZ** is the author of three poetry collections, most recently *Window Left Open* (Graywolf, 2016) and *The Needle* (Houghton Mifflin Harcourt, 2011). She has translated Hubert Haddad's novel *Rochester Knockings: A Novel of the Fox Sisters* (Open Letter, 2015) and Patrice de La Tour du Pin's poetry collection *Psalms of All My Days* (Carnegie Mellon, 2013). She teaches at the University of Rochester.

PIOTR GWIAZDA is the author of three books of poetry—most recently *Aspects of Strangers* (Moria Books, 2015) and *Messages: Poems & Interview* (Pond Road Press, 2012)—and two critical studies, most recently *US Poetry in the Age of Empire, 1979-2012* (Palgrave Macmillan, 2014). He teaches at the University of Maryland Baltimore County.

CHLOE HONUM's poetry collection *The Tulip-Flame* (Cleveland State Univ Poetry Center, 2014) won the Foreword Review's Book of the Year and the Eric Hoffer Book Award. She is the recipient of a Ruth Lilly Fellowship and a Pushcart Prize, and her poems have appeared in *The Paris Review*, *Poetry*, *The Southern Review*, and elsewhere. She was raised in Auckland, New Zealand.

CHRISTOPHER HOWELL is the author of eleven collections of poems, including *Gaze* (Milkweed Editions, 2012) and *Dreamless and Possible: Poems New & Selected* (Univ of Washington Press, 2010). He teaches at Eastern Washington University and in the low-residency MFA program at Eastern Oregon University.

MARK IRWIN is the author of eight collections of poetry, including *American Urn (Selected Poems 1987-2014)* (Ashland Poetry Press, 2015), *Large White House Speaking*

(New Issues, 2013), and *Tall If* (2008). He recently completed a collection of essays on contemporary poetry titled *Monster* and teaches at the University of Southern California.

ELIZABETH LANGEMAK lives in Philadelphia, Pennsylvania.

MICHAEL LEVAN has recent work in *The Boiler Journal, Hobart, Mid-American Review, Ruminator,* and elsewhere. He teaches at the University of Saint Francis, writes reviews for *American Microreviews & Interviews,* and lives in Fort Wayne, Indiana, with his wife, Molly, and their children, Atticus and Dahlia.

DAN MANCILLA is the author of the novella *The Deathmask of El Guacho* (Passages North/Little Presque Books, 2016), and his story collection *All the Proud Fathers* is forthcoming form Dock Street Press. His work has been published in *Barrelhouse, The Chicago Tribune, Monkeybicycle, River Styx,* and elsewhere. He teaches at Aquinas College in Grand Rapids, Michigan.

RANDALL MANN is the author of four poetry collections, including *Straight Razor* (Persea Books, 2013), *Breakfast with Thom Gunn* (Univ of Chicago Press, 2009), which was a finalist for the Lambda Literary Award for Gay Poetry, and the forthcoming *Proprietary* (Persea Books, 2017). Mann lives in San Francisco.

L. S. McKEE's poetry has appeared or is forthcoming in *Blackbird, Crazyhorse, Gulf Coast, Indiana Review,* and elsewhere. Originally from East Tennessee and the recipient of a Wallace Stegner Fellowship, she lives in Atlanta and teaches at the University of West Georgia.

ALEXIS ORGERA is the author of two full-length poetry books: *Dust Jacket* (Coconut Books, 2013) and *How Like Foreign Objects* (H_ngm_n Books 2011). Her poems and nonfiction can be found in *Bat City Review, Black Warrior Review, Gulf Coast, Prairie Schooner,* and elsewhere. She is co-publisher of Penny Candy Books, a press that focuses on equity and variety in children's literature.

ERIC PANKEY's most recent collection of poetry is *Crow-Work* (Milkweed Editions, 2015). He teaches at George Mason University.

ALISON POWELL's first collection of poetry *Desire to Levitate* (Ohio UP, 2014) won the Hollis Summers Poetry Prize. Her work appears or is forthcoming in *Alaska Quarterly Review, American Literary Review,* and *Michigan Quarterly Review.* She teaches poetry at Oakland University.

ANAND PRAHLAD's memoir *The Secret Life of a Black Aspie* is forthcoming from Alaska University Press, and his book of poems is *As Good As Mango* (Stephen F. Austin UP, 2012). In addition, his work appears in *Natural Bridge, Nimrod, Pleiades*, and *Water~Stone Review*. He teaches at the University of Missouri.

CHRISTOPHER SANTIAGO's debut poetry collection *Tula* won the Lindquist & Venum Prize and is forthcoming from Milkweed Editions. He teaches at the University of St. Thomas in St. Paul, Minnesota.

MARTHA SILANO is the author of five books, including *What the Truth Tastes Like* (Two Sylvias Press, 2015), *Reckless Lovely* (Saturnalia Books, 2014), and *The Daily Poet: Day-by-Day Prompts for Your Writing Practice* (Two Sylvias Press, 2013). Poems have appeared recently in *Blackbird, New Ohio Review, Poetry*, and elsewhere. Silano edits *Crab Creek Review* and teaches at Bellevue College.

SHOBA is the sobriquet of Bosnian visual and performance artist Nebojša Šerić, who now lives in New York City. For more information on Shoba, see page 77.

PIOTR SOMMER has published numerous books in his native Poland, including a Collected Poems in 2013, and he has translated many American, British, and Irish poets into Polish, including Frank O'Hara. His poems appear in English translation in the book *Continued* (Wesleyan UP 2005).

EVELYN SOMERS is the recipient of a Barbara Deming Foundation grant, and her work has appears in *Crazyhorse, Georgia Review, Pank, Shenandoah*, and elsewhere. She lives in central Missouri.

MOLLY SPENCER's poetry appears in *Mid-American Review, The Missouri Review, New England Review, ZYZZYVA*, and elsewhere. Her book reviews appear in *The Rumpus* and *Colorado Review*.

SUSAN TICHY is the author of five books, most recently *Trafficke* (Ahsahta Press, 2015)—a mixed-form meditation on family, race, history, and language—*Gallowglass* (2010), and *Bone Pagoda* (2007). She teaches as George Mason University and, when not teaching, lives in a ghost town in southern Colorado.

C. McALLISTER WILLIAMS' poetry collections are *Neon Augury* (Fact-Simile Editions, 2011) and *WILLIAM SHATNER* (alice blue books, 2010). His work appears in *Columbia Poetry Review, ILK, Pinwheel, Sonora Review*, and elsewhere. He lives in Milwaukee and serves as poetry editor for *cream city review*.

NICHOLAS WONG is the author of *Cravasse* (Kaya Press, 2015), winner of the 28th Lambda Literary Award in Gay Poetry. His poems and translations have appeared in *Bellingham Review, diode, Massachusetts Review, The Missouri Review Online*, and *Iron Horse Literary Review*. A "real Asian poet," he lives in Hong Kong, where he serves as an assistant poetry editor for *Drunken Boat*.

Poet, Playwright, and visual artist GRZEGORZ WRÓBLEWSKI grew up in Warsaw and lives in Copenhagen. His most recent works available in English translation are *Let's Go Back to the Mainland* (Červená Barva, 2014) and *Kopenhaga* (Zephyr Press, 2013). For more information on Wróblewski, see page 43.

LIZ WYCKOFF's short fiction has been published in *Quarterly West, Annalemma*, and *The Collagist*, among other journals. Her reviews and interviews have appeared in *The Rumpus, Electric Lit*, and *Tin House* online. She currently lives in Madison, Wisconsin, where she works as an editor.

Required Reading

(Issue 23)

(Each issue we ask that our contributors recommend up to three recent titles. What follows is the list generated by this issue's contributors.)

Floyce Alexander, *The Grand Piano* (Christopher Howell)

Yehuda Amichai, *The Poetry of Yehuda Amichai*, ed. Robert Alter (Landon Godfrey)

Jacob M. Appel, *Miracles and Conundrums of the Secondary Planets* (Okla Elliott)

Emily Apter, *Against World Literature: On the Politics of Untranslatability* (Piotr Gwiazda)

Jeff Baker, *Whoop and Shush* (Jennifer Atkinson)

Dodie Bellamy, *When the Sick Rule the World* (Randall Mann)

Oliver Bendorf, *The Spectral Wilderness* (Anna Barngrover)

Carrie Bennett, *The Land Is a Painted Thing* (Henry Crawford)

David Bergman, *The Poetry of Disturbance: The Discomforts of Postwar American Poetry* (Piotr Gwiazda)

Monica Berlin & Beth Marzoni, *No Shape Bends the River So Long* (Michael Levan)

Reginald Dwayne Betts, *Bastards of the Reagan Era* (Charlie Clark)

Shane Book, *Congotronic* (Adam Chiles)

Alain de Botton, *The Course of Love* (Adrian Blevins)

Anne Boyer, *Garments Against Women* (Alison Powell)

Brennan, Davio, Swift, & Mydlleton-Evans, Eds., *The Poet's Quest for God* (Okla Elliott)

Gwendolyn Brooks, *Blacks* (M. M. Brooks)

Suzanne Buffam, *A Pillow Book* ((Jennifer Grotz)

Anne Carson, *The Albertine Workout* (Elizabeth Langemak)

Melanie Challenger, *On Extinction: How We Became Estranged from Nature* (Martha Silano)

Katie Chase, *Man and Wife* (Liz Wyckoff)

Ta-Nehisi Coates, *Between the World and Me* (M. M. Brooks, Anand Prahlad)

Henri Cole, *Nothing to Declare* (Chloe Honum)

Bernard Cornwell, *The Last Kingdom* Series (George Brookings)

Jonathan Culler, *Theory of the Lyric* (Stephen Burt)

J. K. Daniels, *Wedding Pulls* (Eric Pankey)

Meg Day, *Last Psalm at Sea Level* (L. S. McKee)

Don Delillo, *Zero K* (Mark Irwin)

Lisa Duggan, *The Twilight of Equality* (M. M. Brooks)

Claudia Emerson, *impossible bottle* (Adam Chiles)

Angie Estes, *Enchantée* (Mark Irwin)

Ed Falco, *Toughs* (Stephen Gibson)

Joseph Fasano, *Vincent* (Michael Levan)

Alec Finlay, *Taigh: a wilding garden* (Susan Tichy)

Vievee Francis, *Forest Primeval* (Landon Godfrey)

Zelda Leah Gatuskin, *Digital Face* (Paula Gordon)

Aracelis Girmay, *the black maria* (Michael Levan)

Amelia Gray, *Gutshot* (Liz Wyckoff)

Linda Gregerson, *Prodigal: New & Selected Poems* (Andrew Deloss Eaton)

Jennifer Grotz, *window left open* (Molly Spencer)

John Z. Guzlowski, *Echoes of Tattered Tongues: Memory Unfolded* (Okla Elliott)

Jennifer Haigh, *Heat and Light* (Evelyn Somers)

Barbara Hamby, *On the Streets of Divine Love: New & Selected Poems* (Stephen Gibson)

Gary Hawkins, *Worker* (Landon Godfrey)

Terrance Hayes, *How to Be Drawn* (Anand Prahlad)

Dustin M. Hoffman, *One-Hundred-Knuckled Fist* (Dan Mancilla)

Skip Horack, *The Other Joseph* (L. S. McKee)

Sarah Howe, *Loop of Jade* (Andrew Deloss Eaton)

Brandon Davis Jennings, *Battle Rattle* (Dan Mancilla)

Janine Joseph, *Driving Without a License* (Christopher Santiago)

Fady Joudah, *Textu* (Christopher Santiago)

Bettina Judd, *Patient* (Chloe Honum)

W. Todd Kaneko, *The Dead Wrestler Elegies* (Dan Mancilla, Christopher Santiago)

Laura Kasischke, *The Infinitesimals* (Christopher Howell)

Laura Kasischke, *Space in Chains* (Mark Irwin)

Kim Kyung Ju, *I Am a Season That Does Not Exist in This World*, trans. Jake Levine (Nicholas Wong)

David Kirby, *Get Up, Please* (Stephen Gibson)

Alyse Knorr, *Copper Mother* (Jennifer Atkinson, Eric Pankey)

Melissa Kwasny, *Earth Recitals* (Christopher Howell)

Elad Lassry, *On Onions* (Nicholas Wong)

Keith Leonard, *Ramshackle Ode* (Anna Barngrover, Jennifer Grotz)

Mark Levine, *The Travels of Marco* (Justin Boening)

Robin Coste Lewis, *Voyage of the Sable Venus* (Hannah Craig)

Trudy Lewis, *The Empire Rolls* (Evelyn Somers)

Ada Limón, *Bright Dead Things* (Adrian Blevins)

Valeria Luiselli, *The Story of My Teeth*, trans. Christina MacSweeney (Paula Gordon)

Helen Macdonald, *H Is for Hawk* (Anna Barngrover)

Robert Macfarlane, *Landmarks* (Susan Tichy)

Nathaniel Mackey, *Blue Fasa* (C. McAllister Williams)

Ruth Madievsky, *Emergency Brake* (Alexis Orgera)

Sally Mann, *Hold Still* (Martha Silano)

Nate Marshall, *Wild Hundreds* (Tim Carter)

Dawn Lundy Martin, *Life in a Box Is a Pretty Life* (C. McAllister Williams)

Davis McCombs, *lore* (Chloe Honum)

Lo Kwa Mei-en, *The Bees Make Money in the Lion* (Traci Brimhall)

Thorpe Moeckel, *Arcadia Road: A Trilogy* (Hannah Craig)

Miguel Murphy, *Detainee* (Randall Mann)

Vi Khi Nao, *The Old Philosopher* (John Chávez)

Matthew Neill Null, *Allegheny Front* (Liz Wyckoff)

A. M. O'Malley, *Expecting Something Else* (Alexis Orgera)

Robert Ostrom, *Ritual and Bit* (Justin Boening)

Helen Oyeyemi, *What Is Not Yours Is Not Yours* (Anand Prahlad)

Michael Palmer, *The Laughter of the Sphinx* (Eric Pankey)

Hannah Sanghee Park, *The Same-Different* (Justin Boening)

Soham Patel, *New Weather Drafts* (C. McAllister Williams)

Craig Santos Perez, *From Unincorporated Territory* (John Chávez)

Joshua Poteat, *The Regret Histories* (Adam Chiles, Molly Spencer)

Jana Prikryl, *The After Party* (Charlie Clark, Hannah Craig)

Justin Quinn, *Between Two Fires: Transnationalism and Cold War Poetry* (Piotr Gwiazda)

Sam Quinones, *Dreamland* (L. S. McKee)

Claudia Rankine, *Citizen* (Tim Carter)

Marilynne Robinson, *Loop of Jade* (Andrew Deloss Eaton)

Iliana Rocha, *Karankawa* (Traci Brimhall)

Martha Ronk, *Transfer of Qualities* (Nicholas Wong)

Jason Schneiderman, *Primary Source* (Charlie Clark)

Steve Schreiner, *Belly* (Jennifer Atkinson)

Corinna McClanahan Schroeder, *Inked* (Christopher Santiago)

Adam Schuitema, *Haymaker* (Dan Mancilla)

Sarah Schulman, *Gentrification of the Mind* (M. M. Brooks)

Diane Seuss, *Four-Legged Girl* (Chloe Honum)

Solmaz Sharif, *Look* (Jennifer Grotz)

Laura Sims, *Staying Alive* (C. McAllister Williams)

Magda Szabo, *The Door*, trans. Len Rix (Martha Silano)

Brian Teare, *The Empty Form Goes All the Way to Heaven* (Susan Tichy)

Kelly Thompson & Sophie Campbell, *Jem and the Holograms Vol. One* (Stephen Burt)

Sue Ellen Thompson, *They* (Henry Crawford)

Leo Tolstoy, *Anna Karenina*, trans. Marian Schwartz (Paula Gordon)

Catherynne M. Valente, *Radiance* (Stephen Burt)

Ellen Bryant Voigt, *Headwaters* (Adrian Blevins)

Ocean Vuong, *Night Sky with Exit Wounds* (Traci Brimhall)

C. D. Wright, *The Poet, the Lion, Talking Pictures, El Farolito, a Wedding in St. Roch, the Big Box Store, the Warp in the Mirror, Spring, Midnights, Fire & All* (Molly Spencer)

RED HEN PRESS

cordially invites you to our

22ND

BENEFIT

champagne luncheon

OCTOBER 30, 2016

RECEPTION BEGINS AT 11 A.M.

at

THE WESTIN PASADENA

191 N. LOS ROBLES AVENUE, PASADENA, CA 91101

FEATURING

JILL BIALOSKY   RITA DOVE   ALAN LIGHTMAN

FOR MORE INFO VISIT

WWW.REDHEN.ORG/EVENTS/BENEFIT

Welcome to our new website:
www.laurelreview.org

Sumbmissions	Subscribers	Issues

COPPER NICKEL & MILKWEED EDITIONS
announce

THE JAKE ADAM YORK PRIZE

for a first or second poetry collection

($2,000 + a standard royalty contract
+ publication by Milkweed Editions)

submission deadline:
October 15, 2016

final judge: **ROSS GAY**

for more info:
copper-nickel.org/bookprize/

COPPERNICKEL

subscription rates

For regular folks:

one year (two issues)—$20
two years (four issues)—$35
three years (six issues)—$45
five years (ten issues)—$60

For student folks:

one year (two issues)—$15
two years (four issues)—$23
three years (six issues)—$32
five years (ten issues)—$50

For more information, visit: www.copper-nickel.org.

To go directly to subscriptions
visit: www.regonline.com/coppernickelsubscriptions.

To order back issues, call 303-556-4026
or email wayne.miller@ucdenver.edu.